BIRDS of
GREECE

POCKET PHOTO GUIDES

Rebecca Nason

H E L M

LONDON • OXFORD • NEW YORK • NEW DELHI • SYDNEY

HELM
Bloomsbury Publishing Plc
50 Bedford Square, London, WC1B 3DP, UK

BLOOMSBURY, HELM and the HELM logo are trademarks of
Bloomsbury Publishing Plc

First published in the United Kingdom 2020

A catalogue record for this book is available from the British Library

Library of Congress Cataloguing-in-Publication data has been applied for

ISBN: PB: 978-1-4729-4903-5; eBook: 978-1-4729-4902-8

2 4 6 8 10 9 7 5 3 1

Designed by Susan McIntyre

Printed and bound in India by Replika Press Pvt. Ltd.

MIX
Paper from
responsible sources
FSC® C016779
www.fsc.org

To find out more about our authors and books, visit www.bloomsbury.com
and sign up for our newsletters

CONTENTS

INTRODUCTION

Greece is an extraordinarily beautiful, diverse country, with a pre-dominantly mountainous mainland, an extensive coastline, more than 680 wetlands and an archipelago of more than 2,000 islands. Unlike many European countries, extensive natural and semi-natural habitats remain intact, with Mediterranean forest covering 25–30 per cent of the land area. Alpine, forest and pasture-rich montane habitats abound, while agriculture accounts for most land use. Given Greece's geographical location at the intersection of Europe, Asia and Africa, its diverse range of habitats and its favourable climate of hot summers and cool winters, it is no surprise that the country is very rich in both fauna and flora.

Greece has been a top destination for holidaymakers for decades, attracted by the warm weather, beaches, welcoming inhabitants, fabulous cuisine, and fascinating history and archaeology. But the birdlife is equally spectacular, not least because Greece is a migrant hotspot, situated on the flight path of birds travelling to and from Africa. The country's southerly location also means that many of the diverse resident species are at the northern edge of their range and are not found elsewhere in Europe. In addition, the multitude of freshwater lakes and extensive coastal wetlands in Greece attract a wide range of wintering birds, especially wildfowl and waders.

BIRDLIFE IN GREECE

More than 460 bird species have been recorded in Greece, making it one of the top, still relatively untapped birding destinations in Europe. Recent figures from BirdLife International and the International Union for Conservation of Nature show that 251 species are regularly recorded breeding in Greece; 83 of these species are classed as European birds of conservation concern and 22 are of global conservation concern. More than 40 per cent of the European population of the Near Threatened Dalmatian Pelican live here year-round, and Greece's breeding populations of the Vulnerable Yelkouan Shearwater are ranked second in importance in Europe after Italy. The country is home to 80 percent of the world's population of Eleonora's Falcons. Other important breeding species include Levant Sparrowhawk and Rock Partridge, while significant populations of wintering waterbirds include Common Pochard, Ferruginous Duck and Kentish Plover.

Spring is regarded as the best time for birdwatching in Greece, with migration peaking from late April to early May. Autumn can also be very bountiful, particularly in September. Outside these migration periods, summer and winter visitors – along with populations of the resident Mediterranean species – keep most birdwatchers and photographers entertained.

HOW TO USE THIS BOOK

This handy photographic pocket guide – the first of its kind to cover Greece – describes and depicts nearly 300 of the most likely birds you will encounter while visiting the Greek mainland and its offshore islands. All the common and scarce birds are covered, and a few rarer species are also acknowledged. Although a number of vagrants have been omitted due to lack of space, along with a few rare resident species that have low populations and restricted ranges, this should lessen the likelihood of species confusion and aid identification. Omissions include the wintering populations of the endangered Lesser White-fronted Goose. Breeding birds not included are the rare and restricted populations of Goosander, Capercaillie & Hazel Grouse.

Each species account is illustrated with one or more colour photographs showing the plumages most likely to be seen in Greece, so winter visitors are shown in winter plumage and summer visitors in summer breeding plumage. In most cases, if there are significant differences in male and female plumages, both are illustrated. All the images are of wild birds and have been chosen to highlight the best visible features to aid identification.

The common English name of each species is given next to its scientific name according to the Association of European Records and Rarities Committees Western Palearctic July 2015 list. Also included in the heading is the total body length of the bird, given as a range where there is a significant variation (e.g. between the sexes). The text describes the species' appearance as simply as possible, highlighting the key features and providing separate details for male, female and juvenile where these differ. Comparisons with other species are given when this information is useful. Call and song are highlighted for some species, where appropriate. Finally, the favoured habitat requirements and general distribution of the species in Greece are described, along with information on abundance and seasonality.

The species accounts use technical terms to aid the accurate description of key features. These are depicted in the annotated body and feather illustration below. It is worth familiarising yourself with this terminology as it is used by birdwatchers across the world when describing birds and their features.

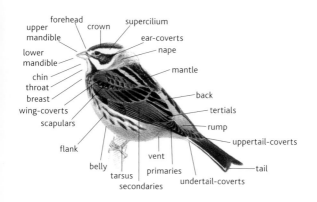

For descriptions of the birds not covered in this pocket guide or for more in-depth information on those that are, the *Collins Bird Guide* is highly recommended (see 'Resources', page 157).

NATURAL GREECE – AN OVERVIEW

Despite Greece's varied birdlife, the country has shown little historical interest in ornithology and its bird-hunting fraternity remains strong. In addition, poor land management and weak regulations have resulted in large-scale abuse and degradation of the natural environment, in particular in the country's prime wetland sites, where drainage is a persistent problem. The country's fauna and flora have suffered as a result, but Greece is slowly awakening to the value of its natural wonders, and its nascent birdwatching and nature tourism market – along with associated habitat and species conservation – is beginning to take shape.

Greece has 10 national parks, 11 Ramsar wetland sites of inter-national importance and 196 Important Bird Areas. The Hellenic Ornithological Society, BirdLife International's partner in Greece, was founded in 1982 and has seen much growth in the last few decades, becoming the main organisation to tackle key nature conservation issues in Greece strongly and effectively. Other bodies, including WWF Greece, have also increased their presence in recent years and boosted public interest and awareness in conservation. The future for birds and wildlife, and the natural areas they inhabit in Greece, is looking more positive than ever, and there has never been a better time for birdwatchers to visit this incredible country.

Most birdwatchers and bird photographers visiting Greece focus on the few classic destinations, such as the islands of Rhodes, Corfu, Crete and Lesvos, along with the northern mainland lakes. While these sites deserve their honeypot status, they are just the tip of the iceberg as far as Greek birdwatching sites go.

TOP BIRDING SITES IN GREECE

What follows is a selection of the best birdwatching locations across the Greek mainland and islands.

1. Lesvos
The Aegean island of Lesvos is one of the top birding destinations in Europe, particularly in spring, when breeding birds are returning and migrants are passing through. An interesting mix of northern European and Mediterranean species occur. Guides and maps to the best birdwatching sites on this welcoming island are readily available (see 'Resources', page 157). Krüper's Nuthatch, Cinereous Bunting, Isabelline Wheatear, Rufous-tailed Scrub Robin, Sombre Tit, Masked Shrike and Olive-tree Warbler are top target species.

2. Crete
The largest island in the south-east Mediterranean is a magnet for migrant birds in spring and autumn, and also home to a rich array of

wintering, resident and breeding species. Top target birds include breeding Eleonora's Falcon, and resident species such as Lammergeier, Bonelli's Eagle, Alpine Chough, Red-billed Chough, Blue Rock Thrush and Zitting Cisticola. Flycatchers, warblers, herons, egrets and crakes pass through in good numbers on passage.

3. Limnos
Smaller and less renowned than Lesvos, the rather flat Aegean island of Limnos can be exceptional for birding, particularly in its eastern areas during the spring migration. The coastal lagoons, lakes, reedbeds and marshes all attract a large array of wetland species, including breeding Ferruginous Duck, Eurasian Stone-curlew, Ruddy Shelduck and Zitting Cisticola. Lesser Kestrel, Cretzschmar's Bunting and Chukar breed inland. Populations of Audouin's Gull and Scopoli's and Yelkouan shearwaters can be found breeding along the coast.

4. Prespa Lakes
The famous Prespa lakes in Greece's north-west (shared by Albania and North Macedonia), along with the surrounding mountains and grassland habitats, are rich in birdlife and have been awarded national park status. Pygmy Cormorant and Dalmatian and Great White pelicans breed on the lakes, and the surrounding habitats come alive with typical Mediterranean species in summer.

5. Nestos Delta
This extensive delta in north-east Greece includes 18 small lakes and eight brackish lagoons. It is excellent for waterbirds, migrant waders and marsh terns, along with Red Kite in winter. Along the river itself, the largest remaining area of riparian forest in Greece (covering more than 400ha) acts as a magnet for raptors. Further inland, the impressive, well-vegetated Nestos Gorge forms a natural boundary between North Macedonia and Thrace. Raptors hunt along the gorge, the dense understorey is alive with breeding warblers in spring and Spur-winged Plover summer in the area.

6. Porto Lagos, Lake Vistonida and Lake Ismarida
This sprawling network of brackish lagoons and freshwater lakes lies in north-east Greece. Lake Vistonida is well known for wintering Black-necked Grebe and White-headed Duck, and is a good site for Slender-billed Gull, Spur-winged Plover, Pygmy Cormorant and Greater Flamingo. Porto Lagos attracts concentrations of wintering gulls, Dalmatian Pelican and egrets. The local saltworks teem with waders and terns in spring, and the surrounding fields are excellent for various shrikes, buntings, larks and Collared Pratincole.

7. Mt Parnassus
A popular tourist destination in winter, this limestone mountain is a very important site for many forest and alpine birds in all seasons. Black Woodpecker, Rock Partridge, Sombre Tit, Golden Eagle, Common Rock Thrush and Blue Rock Thrush are resident, and the area teems with commoner Mediterranean species in summer.

8. Lake Kerkini

Artificial Lake Kerkini, 100km north of Thessaloniki on the northern mainland, is one of the most important wetlands in Europe. It is rich in birdlife year-round, but is perhaps best visited in spring as the breeding season gets underway, with species returning from Africa, and ducks and geese arriving to escape the harsher weather further north. It is the most important site in Europe for the globally endangered Dalmatian Pelican.

9. Evros Delta

Situated in north-eastern Greece, the broad Evros Delta attracts vast numbers of wetland birds, making the site a top Greek birdwatching destination year-round. It is also on the main migratory route for many species. Winter sees large numbers of Greater White-fronted Goose, Ruddy Shelduck, Dalmatian Pelican, Pygmy Cormorant, Grey Heron and Little Egret. Summer highlights include Black Stork, Great White Pelican, Purple Heron, Glossy Ibis, Greater Flamingo and various waders and terns.

10. Dadia Forest

Tucked into the mountainous north-east, Dadia Forest is one of the best raptor hotspots in Europe. It is the only breeding site in Greece for Cinereous Vulture, a species with a very restricted range in Europe. Griffon Vulture, Golden Eagle, Black Kite and Long-legged Buzzard are other resident highlights. Egyptian Vulture, Lesser Spotted Eagle, Short-toed Eagle, Booted Eagle and Levant Sparrowhawk are regularly seen in summer, and White-tailed Eagle, Eastern Imperial Eagle and Great Spotted Eagle in winter.

11. Mt Olympus

In addition to its stunning array of plant and butterfly species, Mt Olympus is home to some of Greece's rarer resident montane bird species and a host of commoner woodland species. Birds that can be seen year-round include Black Woodpecker, White-backed Woodpecker, Alpine Chough, Crested Tit and Rock Bunting. Rarer resident summit species include Alpine Accentor.

12. Ambracian Gulf and Rodia Wetlands

The northern parts of this enormous wetland in western Greece are the most productive for birdlife. The famous Rodia Lagoon is a hotspot for thousands of ducks in winter, many wetland species occur year-round and the spring passage migration can be spectacular. Dalmatian Pelican breed here, and the marshes teem with herons, egrets, waders and terns in spring. Caspian Tern and Gull-billed Tern may also be seen, as can passing marsh terns. The nearby mountains are good for raptors, owls and many commoner woodland species

13 & 14. The Peloponnese

A large peninsula in the south of the country connected to the rest of mainland Greece via the Isthmus of Corinth land bridge, the

Peloponnese has two must-visit Important Bird Areas. The first, in the north-west (**13**), comprises Kotychi Lagoon and Kalogria Lagoon, which are separated by the pine and oak Strofylia Forest. The marshes and lagoons attract large numbers of migrating waders and terns in spring, and support many ducks – particularly Common Pochard – in the winter. This season also sees flocks of Bearded Reedling on the reedbeds. The other Important Bird Area in the Peloponnese that is particularly worth a visit is Gialova Lagoon (**14**), adjacent to Navarino Bay in the south-west. A fabulous wetland, it is best in winter for ducks and in spring for migrant waders, pipits, wagtails and returning breeding species.

15 & 16. Athens
Two Important Bird Areas lie within a short drive of the capital. Schinias Marsh (**15**), in the Bay of Marathonas 45km from Athens, is a coastal marsh enclosed by sand-dune remnants, pine forest and bird-rich scrub-covered hills. It attracts passage migrants in spring and autumn, and hosts an array of wetland species and raptors in winter. Mt Hymettus (**16**) and the surrounding rocky terrain are a short drive south of Athens. This beautiful area is awash with common breeding Mediterranean species in summer, including various warblers, wheatears and buntings.

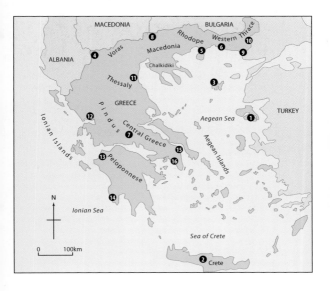

▲ Adult female

▲ Adult male   ▲ Juvenile

MUTE SWAN *Cygnus olor* 145–160cm

Very large all-white swan with a rounded head and very long, curved neck. Bill chunky, orange with black edging, black triangular base and black knob at forehead. Legs thick, short and black. Ungainly on land but graceful on water, with S-shaped neck and head often angled down. Juvenile shows washed-out grey-brown plumage and a pale greyish-pink bill lacking knob. Breeds on fresh waters, favouring reedbeds and coastal fringes; found in more open habitats in winter. Solitary nester. Can make aggressive hissing noises and snorts. Scarce local resident in north-west mainland Greece; locally common winter visitor, with a patchy, mainly coastal mainland, distribution.

WHOOPER SWAN *Cygnus cygnus* 145–160cm

Very large all-white swan with a flattened forehead and long, straight neck. Adult shows sloping black bill with large wedge-shaped yellow patch extending from bill base to nostril and beyond (not seen in adult Bewick's Swan). Legs and feet thick and dark. In profile, swims with neck held high and straight. Juvenile grey-brown, greyer than juvenile Mute Swan, with pinkish-yellow bill and black border to lower mandible. Found mainly on freshwater bodies but also grazes on arable fields and flooded grasslands. Regular local winter visitor, mainly around the Evros Delta.

▼ Juveniles (first winter)   ▶ Adult

TUNDRA SWAN *Cygnus columbianus* 115–127cm

The subspecies in Greece is Bewick's Swan. Very large white swan, smaller than Mute and Whooper swans. Best separation feature from Whooper is the bill, which is less straight and shows a rounded, less extensive yellow patch. Head is rounder and neck shorter than in Whooper. Juvenile greyish, resembling juvenile Whooper. Call is more honking, higher pitched and less repetitive than that of Whooper. Highly gregarious in winter, when large concentrations can be found in suitable open-water habitats. Once rare, now an increasingly regular winter visitor, particularly around the Evros Delta.

GREATER WHITE-FRONTED GOOSE *Anser albifrons* 65–78cm

Distinct medium-sized, compact grey-brown goose, the commonest goose in Greece. Easily identified by broad white blaze surrounding base of bill and forehead, and varying amounts of dark barring on underparts. Bill pinkish, legs and feet rich orange. Juvenile lacks white forehead and barring on underparts, but bill is pink with a dark tip. Feeds on natural grasslands and arable land. Fairly common but local winter visitor between November and March, mainly to the Evros Delta, Thrace and Macedonia, where thousands can gather. Can be found further south around the Aegean Islands in severe winters.

RUDDY SHELDUCK *Tadorna ferruginea* 61–67cm

Medium-sized, rather goose-like duck, with a small black bill and proportionally long legs and neck. Adult has striking burnt-orange body plumage ending halfway up neck, then warm cream around upper neck and head. White around forehead and face highlight small black bill and black button eyes. Male shows distinctive black ring around neck (lost in winter), and a glossy green sheen to black primary feathers and tail. In flight, shows white and black wings from above and below. Juvenile similar but with paler fawny-brown mantle and back. Declining scarce breeder and local partial migrant in Greece. Low numbers breed along north-east coasts of Macedonia and Thrace, south to some Aegean islands. Occurs irregularly on northern mainland coasts in winter.

COMMON SHELDUCK *Tadorna tadorna* 58–67cm

The size and shape of a small goose but with distinctive plumage. Adult of both sexes mainly white with contrasting dark green (almost black) head and neck, broad chestnut-brown breast-band, and black shoulders, flight feathers and central belly stripe. Bill large, bright red-pink and legs bubblegum pink. In summer, male has a bulbous red-pink knob on bill base, rising onto forehead. Juvenile whiter throughout, with grey-brown face, hindneck, back and wings. Bill and legs greyish pink. Calls include a smothered whistle and nasal *ga-ga-ga*. Prefers coasts, mudflats, marshes and some freshwater wetlands. Breeding is patchy, with a northern coastal bias. Fairly scarce local resident; widespread and locally common winter visitor.

▲ Adult males

▲ Adult females

EURASIAN WIGEON *Anas penelope* 45–51cm

Most common wintering duck in Greece. Male distinct, with a rounded chestnut-red head, creamy-yellow forehead, pale blue bill with a black tip, dusky-pink neck, grey body and black rear. White patch on upperwing obvious in flight. Female best identified by shape, with a rounded head, distinctive bill, short neck and pointed tail. Plumage brown, rather mottled, with some orange-brown to breast and flanks, but very variable. Whitish belly evident when feeding on land; lacks white wing-patch. Male in eclipse resembles female but retains white wing-patch. Call is a whistling *wheeooo*. Fairly widespread, locally very common visitor to coastal waters and marshes in winter.

GADWALL *Anas strepera* 46–56cm

Medium-sized dabbling duck, smaller and slimmer than Mallard. Male finely speckled grey, with a browner head and conspicuous black rear. White speculum and chestnut wing-coverts obvious in flight. Bill dark grey. Female like female Mallard, but has orange sides to bill, colder-toned plumage, white speculum in flight and white on belly. Juvenile like female but richer brown, with no obvious white speculum in flight. Often found in pairs on large wetlands, lakes, and brackish and freshwater habitats with ample vegetation. Scarce local resident in northern Greece; fairly common winter visitor along coastal mainland Greece. Evros Delta holds the largest wintering population, and Macedonia and Thrace together hold the core resident breeding population.

 Adult male ▲ Adult female

EURASIAN TEAL *Anas crecca* 34–38cm

Shy, small dabbling duck. Male pale grey with fine black flecks throughout and a dark-speckled buff breast. Distinctive chestnut head with broad, metallic green eye-patch bordered by thin cream lines. Also a black-bordered yellow undertail triangle and narrow black-and-white horizontal stripe along wing. Female and juvenile rather featureless, with pale-fringed cold brown feathering throughout, appearing mottled. Both show a small white streak to side of tail base and often some orange to bill base. All show a broad white bar and black-and-green speculum to wings during fast and erratic flight. Male calls with a thin, far-reaching whistle; female has more quacking notes. Very common and widespread winter visitor to coastal wetlands of Greece, often in high concentrations.

MALLARD *Anas platyrhynchos* 50–65cm

Familiar large, stocky dabbling duck. Male has a glossy green head, yellowish-green bill, narrow white collar, rusty-brown breast, greyish body and black-and-white rear. Female mainly mottled buff-brown, with broad, buff-fringed, dark brown feathering throughout and unevenly marked orange-and-brown bill. Both sexes show a blue-purple speculum bordered above and below by a narrow black and a broad white bar, very clear across secondaries in flight. Plumage in eclipse male varied, more like female. Tolerates human presence more than other ducks. The commonest breeding duck in Greece, found in small numbers throughout most wetlands in north and central mainland areas and several islands. Very common, widespread winter visitor.

▼ Adult female (left), adult male (right)

▲ *Adult male* ▲ *Adult female*

NORTHERN PINTAIL *Anas acuta* 51–66cm

Large, slender, long-necked dabbling duck. Male has distinctive long, pointed black central tail feathers, greyish plumage, a rich brown head and neck, and a white breast extending up hindneck in a narrow stripe. Dark speculum bordered by white trailing edge and orange front edge in flight. Bill pale grey and black. Female scalloped buff and brown throughout, with a rather plain face, pale underbelly and dark chevrons through white undertail. Bill dark grey. Narrow white trailing edge and wing-bar in flight, pointed tail, long neck and small head should dispel Mallard at a distance. Favours brackish and saline coastal lagoons. Rare breeder in northern Greece. Very common, widespread winter visitor and passage migrant throughout coastal Greece and some islands.

GARGANEY *Anas querquedula* 37–41cm

Shy, small dabbling duck with a proportionally long, slim bill. Male distinctive, with a bold white supercilium, chocolate-brown crown, finely speckled brown face and breast, and pale grey-and-white flank-patch. Scapulars with long plume-like black-and-white feathers, and rear pale buff with fine dark spotting. Female similar to Eurasian Teal female, but with pale buff patch to bill base and throat, and buff-brown face with contrasting dark brown crown-, eye- and cheek-stripes. Found in freshwater wetlands. Breeds in very small numbers in scattered locations, mainly in Macedonia and Thrace. Scarce local summer visitor; common and widespread passage migrant. Very common on migration, especially in spring throughout wetlands of mainland Greece and most islands.

▼ *Adult male* ▼ *Adult female*

 ▲ Adult male ▲ Adult female

NORTHERN SHOVELER *Anas clypeata* 44–52cm

Short-necked, medium-sized dabbling duck, the size of a Mallard, with a very distinctive large spatula-shaped bill in both sexes. Male has a dark green head, white underparts, and a rich chestnut belly and flank-patch. Back black with elongated black-and-white feathers along scapulars. Forewing is powder blue, obvious in flight. Female and juvenile similar to Mallard female, with mottled brown plumage throughout, pale grey forewing and white underwing, and orange-brown bill. Overall shape and weighty spatula bill make for straightforward identification, even for eclipse male and juvenile. Found in coastal wetlands, open marshes and freshwater lakes. Fairly widespread and common winter visitor to northern Greece; passage migrant.

RED-CRESTED POCHARD *Netta rufina* 53–57cm

Shy, large dabbling duck with a bulky body and top-heavy rounded head. Male has a burnt-orange head and strong red bill. Upperparts brown; neck, breast, belly and rear black; flanks white. Female and juvenile brown throughout but with top half of head brown and bottom half whitish grey. Bill grey with pink spot at tip in adult female. Both sexes show broad white wing-bar in flight. Eclipse male looks more like a red-brown version of adult female with red-pink bill and red eye. Prefers freshwater lakes, coastal bays and saline marshes. Regular but scarce winter visitor to northern and western mainland wetlands.

▼ Adult male ▼ Adult female

▲ *Adult males* ▲ *Adult female*

COMMON POCHARD *Aythya ferina* 42–49cm

Medium-sized diving duck with a high crown, gently sloping forehead and longish broad bill, giving it a distinctive profile. Male has chestnut head and neck, red eye, blue-grey band across dark bill and pale grey body, contrasting with black breast and rear. Female has grey-brown body with mid-brown head, neck and rear, and paler brown spectacles and lore patch. Juvenile shows all-dark bill and more uniform pale brown plumage. In flight, wings lack strong contrast, appearing uniform grey. Prefers open, coastal freshwater lakes and brackish lagoons and marshes. Very rare and local resident; common and widespread winter visitor, particularly in the north and west mainland.

FERRUGINOUS DUCK *Aythya nyroca* 38–42cm

Small, compact diving duck with a flat forehead and high rear crown. Male mahogany brown with contrasting white eye, darker brown back, and clear-cut white belly-patch and undertail. Female similar but lacks chestnut tones to brown plumage and has a dark eye. Juvenile cooler brown, with whitish belly and undertail. In flight, all show broad white wing-bar to upperwing. Favours well-vegetated freshwater wetlands and marshes. Scarce, isolated local breeder; widespread and fairly common passage migrant. Dramatic declines in recent years due to hunting and habitat loss.

▼ *Adult male* ▼ *Adult female*

 ▲ *Adult male*

▲ *Adult female*

TUFTED DUCK *Aythya fuligula* 40–47cm

Fairly small, crested diving duck. Male very black and white, with black crest, head and body contrasting with well-defined white flanks and belly. Black head has violet gloss in good light. Female rich brown throughout, darker on upperparts, paler and mottled along flanks, with short brown crest. Both have golden-yellow eyes, a blue-grey bill with paler grey band near black tip and, in flight, obvious white wing-bars. Juvenile duller brown throughout, with pale brown eye and whitish belly. Female and juvenile often show small white patch at bill base. Prefers richly vegetated freshwater marshes and brackish coastal lagoons. Widespread, common winter visitor to wetlands of west and north mainland Greece.

COMMON GOLDENEYE *Bucephala clangula* 42–50cm

▲ *Adult male*
▼ *Adult female*

Fairly dumpy diving duck with a large rounded head and peaked crown. Male unmistakable, with a black-and-white body, dark green-black head and large white lore spot. Golden eye visible at close range. Female greyish brown with contrasting chocolate-brown head, white wing-patch and collar, pale golden eye and orange-tipped grey bill. Juvenile similar to female but duller grey-brown, and with brown eye and no white collar. All show white innerwing panels in flight. Prefers open freshwater lakes and brackish coastal lagoons. Scarce local winter visitor, with patchy north mainland bias.

▲ Adult male   ▲ Adult female

GREATER SCAUP *Aythya marila* 42–51cm

Larger than Tufted Duck, with a rounder head and no crest. Male has a well-defined black head (often showing a green sheen), breast and rear. Flank-sides white and back white with fine grey barring (back black in male Tufted Duck). Eye yellow and bill greyish blue with a very small black tip and no pale band. Poorly marked female and juvenile are trickier to tell from female Tufted Duck, but have variable, often obvious large white patches around bill base. Adult female has subtle grey tones to brown back and flanks. All have white wing-panels in flight. Scarce winter visitor to north and north-east Greece, with small numbers annually at Lake Kerkini and Lake Vistonida.

SMEW *Mergus albellus* 38–44cm

Small 'sawbill', only marginally bigger than Eurasian Teal. Slender body and neat head with a steep forehead and slight crown. Well-defined plumage in both sexes. Male shows clean black-and-white plumage with pale grey flanks. Head white with small black face-patch and black nape-stripe. Female and juvenile show rufous-brown head, contrasting with large white patch around cheek and throat, pale grey body and white underbelly. Both have small, compact grey bills and obvious white wing-panels in flight. Eclipse male has diffused warm brown area to black-and-white head and greyer wings. Favours open freshwater lakes and coastal lagoons. Scarce local winter visitor, with numbers fluctuating annually.

▼ Adult male   ▶ Adult female

▲ Adult male

▲ Adult female

RED-BREASTED MERGANSER *Mergus serrator* 52–58cm

Largish, slender-bodied 'sawbill' with a bright red bill that is noticeably much thinner, longer and more serrated than in other ducks. Male intricately patterned, with a black-green head, crest and upper neck, white neck collar, buff upper breast peppered with dark spots, and a bright red eye. Back and sides of lower breast black, the latter with a small cluster of white patches. Wings white, flanks and tail pale grey. Female and juvenile similar, but head, crest and upper neck orange-brown, and body plumage uniform grey-brown. Eclipse male resembles female but has a large white wing-patch. Found mainly in inshore waters, sheltered bays and brackish lagoons. Fairly common and widespread winter visitor throughout coastal Greece.

WHITE-HEADED DUCK *Oxyura leucocephala* 43–48cm

Small, stiff-tailed diving duck with a distinctive shape. Male has a white head with a narrow black cap, and large powder-blue bill with a broad, swollen base extending onto forehead. Warm brown above and below, with stronger rust brown to breast and tail base. Tail spike and neck collar black. Female and juvenile duller, grey-billed and uniform brown above and below. White face dominated by diffuse dark horizontal cheek-stripe and extensive dark crown. Frequents richly vegetated lakes. Rare but regular local winter visitor in northern Greece; Lake Vistonida is a traditional stronghold. Numbers fluctuate annually.

▼ Adult male   ▼ Adult female

CHUKAR PARTRIDGE *Alectoris chukar* 32–34cm

Portly, medium-sized partridge. Black band extends from bill across eye, down through cheek, neck-sides and across breast, forming a necklace. Lower face and 'bib' cream. Brown streak behind red-rimmed eye. Mantle, breast and uppertail pale grey-blue. Underparts and undertail washed-out clay brown, and flank-patch white with angled black barring. Bill and legs red. Flight short, low and gliding. Favours bare, stony hillsides, arable farmland and grasslands in both mountain and lowland terrains. Fairly widespread, locally common resident, mainly on islands. Released en masse throughout mainland Greece and islands by the hunting fraternity, resulting in colonisation and interbreeding with native populations.

ROCK PARTRIDGE *Alectoris graeca* 32–35cm

Similar to Chukar in appearance, but distinguished by its cleaner, sharper face and throat pattern, smaller brown streak behind eye, and white (not cream) lower face and throat 'bib'. Black band from bill runs around whole bill base. Bill, legs and eye-ring red. Upperparts greyer and angled flank barring narrower than on Chukar. Primarily an upland species but also found at lower altitudes. Fairly common and widespread resident across mainland Greece and some islands. Popular gamebird, intensely hunted and increasingly shy as a result.

GREY PARTRIDGE *Perdix perdix* 29–31cm

Shy, small rotund partridge, often found in small groups called coveys. Attractive plumage, with an orange-tan face and throat, dainty grey bill, chestnut bars on flanks, and pale grey breast with arched dark chestnut belly-patch, the latter visible only when bid stands upright. Sexes similar, although male more strongly patterned. Juvenile very different, not unlike adult Common Quail or young pheasant, with fine brown, black and white streaking throughout plumage, unmarked pale belly, dark ear-coverts and brown bill. Fairly uncommon resident of cultivated habitats, usually in lowland areas throughout northern Greece. Formerly much more widespread.

COMMON QUAIL *Coturnix coturnix* 16–18cm

Tiny rotund gamebird, with streaky warm brown plumage and an intricate head pattern of dark brown and pale cream stripes. Back and flanks finely marked throughout, with black-edged white and cream streaks. Male shows variable black central throat-patch; female has pale throat. Rarely seen out in the open, more likely heard singing or seen briefly when flushed. Song is a very liquid, sharp *wit'wit'wit*; call is often a soft *wrree*. Breeds on open farmland and grasslands. Fairly common and widespread summer visitor and passage migrant to mainland Greece and most of the islands. More common on autumn passage than in spring.

▲ Adult summer

▲ Adult winter

RED-THROATED DIVER *Gavia stellata* 53–69cm

Thick-necked and longer-bodied than ducks and grebes, and with a strong, dagger-like upturned grey bill and rather flat forehead. Summer plumage (rare in Greece) very distinctive, with long red neck-patch, bright red eye, pale grey neck, darker grey back, and vertical fine black-and-white stripes along back of neck and shoulder. Adult winter and juvenile show dark grey upperparts, hindneck and crown, and white through lower face, throat, neck and underparts. Dark back finely speckled white, and small dark eye usually prominent on white face. Juvenile duskier, with less white on face. Legs set far back, projecting well past body in flight. Increasingly regular winter visitor around coastal offshore waters in north and west Greece.

BLACK-THROATED DIVER *Gavia arctica* 58–73cm

Slightly larger than Red-throated Diver. In winter at a distance, best separated by bulkier head shape, with distinctive steep forehead and blunt-ended peaked crown. Chest appears full and projects forward from body, and bill is deeper and lacks Red-throated's upturned angle. Rare summer adult very distinctive, with grey head and hindneck, black neck-patch, and black and white stripes along sides of neck and shoulder. Large chequered black-and-white patches on back. In winter, two-toned like Red-throated, but white does not envelop eye. Distinctive white patch on hindflanks often a good identification feature. Common winter visitor to offshore waters of northern Greece.

▲ Summer plumage ▲ Winter plumage

LITTLE GREBE *Tachybaptus ruficollis* 25–29cm

Small grebe with a short neck, tiny bill and rather dumpy, blunt-ended body. Summer adult has a rich chestnut cheek and foreneck; brownish-black cap, neck and back; and paler brown-and-white fluffed-up 'powder-puff' appearance at rear. Distinctive fleshy yellow gape at bill base apparent even at a distance. Winter adult shows very light buff-brown on flanks, breast, foreneck and cheeks, darker on back and crown. Juvenile has black-tipped yellow bill, and black and white streaks on cheeks and neck-sides. Breeding widespread, in well-vegetated freshwater lakes; inhabits more open lakes, reservoirs and saline coastal areas in winter. Locally common resident throughout Greece.

GREAT CRESTED GREBE *Podiceps cristatus* 46–51cm

Largest European grebe. Long slender body and dainty neck give it a rather graceful appearance. Summer adult striking, with chestnut-and-black head plumes, held down when at ease but dramatically fanned and shaken during courtship display. Upperparts grey-brown, underparts and face white, and bill slim, pointed and dark pink. Winter adult shows dark brown crown, hindneck and upperparts, and clean white face, eye surround, neck and upper breast. Underparts pale taupe-brown, bill pale pink. Juvenile like winter adult but with broken dark streaking through white face. Courtship involves synchronised water dancing with breast-to-breast contact. Favours reedbed habitats, lakes and reservoirs in summer, and offshore coastal areas in winter. Widespread, locally common resident; common winter visitor.

▼ Adult summer ▼ Adult winter

▲ Summer plumage ▲ Winter plumage

RED-NECKED GREBE *Podiceps grisegena* 40–50cm

Fairly large grebe, similar to Great-crested Grebe but smaller, with a stockier neck and stouter bill. Very distinctive in summer, with a rich red-brown neck, large dusky-washed white cheek and throat-patch, neat black crown enveloping dark eye, and dark bill with yellow base. Crown and back dark, flanks and rear whitish grey with varying dark streaks. Winter adult similar but duller, with diffuse smoky brown through ear-coverts and upper-neck band. Juvenile more like summer adult, but with dark streaking through white face and duskier underparts. Prefers large open waterbodies and inshore coastal waters in winter, and reedbeds and well-vegetated lakes in summer. Scarce local winter visitor to north-east Greece.

BLACK-NECKED GREBE *Podiceps nigricollis* 28–34cm

Small, dainty grebe with a steeply angled forehead and powder-puff rear. Unmistakable in summer, with black upperparts, head, neck and breast contrasting with chestnut-brown underparts and striking golden-yellow ear-tufts, and bright red eye. Winter adult and juvenile dusky brown above and whitish below, with a ruby-red eye. In winter, differs from rare Horned Grebe (*P. auritus*; not illustrated) in that dark brown crown spills behind and below eye, interrupting neat white face-patch. Breeds in small numbers in north mainland, notably at Lake Kerkini. One of the commonest waterbirds in winter, well distributed in coastal waters, lakes and lagoons.

▼ Adult summer ▼ Adult winter

▲ Adult

▲ Adult in flight

SCOPOLI'S SHEARWATER *Calonectris diomedea* 45–56cm

Large, heavy, big-headed seabird, with long wings and rather pale grey-brown upperparts and white underparts. Upperparts diffused grey-brown, with pale feather edges creating scaling pattern along back and rump. Upperwing and tail-end darker brown, with variable narrow white band bordering tail base. Underwing white with dark brown borders. Straight, tubular bill yellow with dark band near tip. Long, stiff wings often held in a 'bowed' position. Flight relaxed, with long glides low over water surface and occasional effortless wingbeats. Often observed at distance, by seawatching from land or boat. Widespread and locally common summer visitor. Breeds colonially in burrows on Dionysades Islets off north-east Crete and other remote rocky islands.

YELKOUAN SHEARWATER *Puffinus yelkouan* 30–36cm

Medium-sized dusky shearwater, smaller and slimmer-winged than Scopoli's Shearwater, with toes projecting past rather short tail. Dusky brown (almost black) above and white below, with lightly diffused dusky breast-sides, flanks, vent and undertail, and variable dark armpit markings. White underwing with obvious dark borders. Long, dark tubular bill. Commonly seen in flight, twisting over waves or in 'rafts' on the surface. Flight often a mix of fast, stiff, straight wingbeats, gliding and banking, alternately revealing dark upperparts and white underparts. Breeds colonially in burrows on coastal cliffs and islands. Comes ashore at night. Fairly common and widespread resident. Seen year-round offshore, most commonly during spring migration.

▲ Adult

▲ Adult in flight

GREAT CORMORANT *Phalacrocorax carbo* 80–100cm

Larger and more robust than European Shag, with a strong, long bill and sloping forehead, peaking at rear. Summer adult black with a bronzy sheen; wings with dark-edged feathering, creating scaly appearance. Yellow skin patch at bill base and white throat-patch are striking. Crown and hindneck have variable white feathers that decrease during summer, and an obvious white hindflank-patch evident just through breeding season. Winter adult duller, lacks gloss, and white areas around face duskier and less defined. Juvenile dull brown on upperparts; underparts off-white, aside from brown streaking to throat and upper breast. Swims very low in the water and dives for large fish. Very upright, erect profile on land. Colonial nester along rocky coasts. Fairly widespread, locally common resident; common and widespread winter visitor.

EUROPEAN SHAG *Phalacrocorax aristotelis* 65–80cm

Smaller than Great Cormorant, with more slender body and bill, and smaller, rounded head and steep forehead. Adult shows blackish plumage throughout, with glossy green sheen and darker-edged 'scaling' to wing feathers at close range. Prominent yellow 'gape' at bill base and short, erect dark crest often visible in early summer. Eye emerald green, bill yellowish, legs dark. Winter adult similar but duller. Juvenile washed-out brown with variable white around throat, neck and underparts. Low profile in water; upright on land, often holding wings out to dry. Nests mainly on coastal cliffs and caves in loose colonies. Common, fairly widespread resident, particularly in northern Greece.

▼ Adult summer   ▼ Adult summer drying wings

PYGMY CORMORANT
Phalacrocorax pygmeus 45–55cm

Long-tailed seabird with distinctly small, rounded head and short, stout bill. Summer adult has green-bronze gloss on dark (almost black) plumage, and varying fine white streaky feathers on head, neck and underparts during breeding period. Winter adult and juvenile show whitish chin and paler brown head and underparts. Breeds in fresh-water wetlands and winters in coastal wetlands. Low profile while swimming and diving for small fish, upright stance on land. Scarce local resident in northern Greece; winter visitor, restricted to larger wetlands in Thrace and Macedonia.

DALMATIAN PELICAN *Pelecanus crispus* 160–180cm

Huge, heavy white waterbird with a broad head and body, long neck and enormous bill with a deep pouch. Tail and legs short. Adult has red-orange bill-pouch and yellow patch on breast. Eyes small and pale, with limited pale skin surround. Legs grey, white body plumage often tinged grey. Immature birds have pale pinkish or yellow bills. Juvenile has brown-grey upperparts and off-white plumage below. All ages have dark blackish wing-tips, clearly visible only in flight. Frequents shallow lakes, swamps, inland waters and lagoons. Gregarious species, feeding and breeding in groups. Fairly common but local resident; the biggest breeding concentration in the world is in northern Greece.

GREAT WHITE PELICAN *Pelecanus onocrotalus* 140–175cm

Very large white waterbird with a huge bill and bill-pouch. Adult white with faint pinkish-yellow tinge, particularly around foreneck during breeding season. Large, dull yellow bill-pouch (brighter when breeding) below pinkish-grey bill. Obvious pink skin patches around dark button eyes. Legs with varying degrees of pinkish-yellow tones, reddish in summer adult. Juvenile with dirty grey-and-white plumage, but pink patches around eyes and yellow bill-pouch present. Extensive black on underwing (obvious in flight) easily distinguishes it from Dalmatian Pelican at a distance. Frequents same habitat as Dalmatian. Scarce local summer visitor and passage migrant.

LITTLE BITTERN *Ixobrychus minutus* 33–38cm

Small, secretive heron, the size of a Common Moorhen. Male has a smart black crown and upperparts, with contrasting cream-buff wing-patches. Underparts cream-buff and white, with pale streaking through breast. Legs yellow, bill deep yellow with black tip. Female has dark crown and upperparts, with pale streaks to back feathers and more rufous-brown on face and neck. Underparts densely streaked brown through throat, breast and flanks. Juvenile brown, streaked darker on upperparts and with blackish crown. Flight call a *kwek*; song (at night) a continuous low croaking. Favours reedbeds and fringes of rivers, lakes, pools, streams and artificial water habitats. Very widespread, common summer visitor and passage migrant.

▼ *Adult female*   ▼ *Adult male in flight*

BLACK-CROWNED NIGHT HERON *Nycticorax nycticorax* 58–65cm

Stocky medium-sized heron with a large head and thick neck. Adult beautifully marked, with a strong black bill, short pale legs, and a black crown and back. Wings pale grey, contrasting with uniform white forehead-band, face, throat and underparts. Large red eye visible at close range, and long white hindcrown plumes rest over back. Juvenile very different, with brown upperparts spotted with white teardrops; underparts buff with brown streaking, denser on breast; bill and legs dull yellow-green. Various croak-like calls. Most active at night; roosts in loose tree colonies by day. Frequents margins of lakes, pools, ponds, rivers, lagoons, streams and some artificial freshwater habitats. Common summer visitor and passage migrant.

SQUACCO HERON *Ardeola ralloides* 44–47cm

Relatively small, pale buffish-brown heron. Conspicuous white wings, rump and tail visible in flight. Summer adult shows clean white below, with pale yellow-buff across breast-sides and wings. Upperparts dusky pink-buff; head covered with fine black and white stripes, extending into long crown plumes over back. Strong, long bill pale blue with black tip. Legs reddish during courtship, otherwise yellow. Winter adult and juvenile very different, with extensive brown and buff streaking through head, neck and breast-sides; dusky brown above, white below. Feet and bill dull yellow. Breeds in small colonies along vegetated water margins. Frequents lowland wetlands, lakes, rivers, vegetated ditches and shallow fresh waters. Common but local summer visitor; widespread, common passage migrant.

LITTLE EGRET *Egretta garzetta* 55–65cm

Medium-sized snow-white heron of slight build, with long, thin, curved neck, long black legs and distinctive yellow feet. Bill is long, straight and dark, with pink-grey lower mandible base and pale yellow-grey lores at close range. Lores pinker during courtship, when long white crown plumes also evident. Mostly silent; call is a harsh, flat note. Common around coasts and inland waters, particularly lakes, pools, ponds, lagoons, slow rivers and streams. Also found in brackish estuaries and saline waters, saltpans, irrigated areas and floodplains. Breeds in small colonies within reedbeds, thickets and trees. Common and widespread resident and passage migrant, most numerous in spring.

GREAT EGRET *Egretta alba* 85–102cm

Large, pure white heron, similar in size to Grey Heron, with a long, thin, curved neck, long legs and a strong, long bill. Feet black (yellow in Little Egret). Non-breeding adult and juvenile have dark legs with yellowish upper tibia and obvious yellow bill. Summer adult has bill black with yellow base, and long white tail and breast plumes. Flight rather lethargic, with head and neck retracted, and long legs extending beyond tail. Quite solitary, but breeds in large heronries in summer. Found in lowland freshwater and saltwater marshes, estuaries, rivers, lagoons and ditches. Scarce local resident in northern Greece; widespread, common and increasing winter visitor.

GREY HERON *Ardea cinerea* 90–98cm

Large, robust heron with a slender body, long legs and neck, heavy dagger-like yellow bill, and grey-and-white plumage. Adult has a white head, neck and underparts, with a prominent black stripe (actually a plume) behind eye and varying fine black vertical streaks running through central neck and breast. Wings, back and tail storm grey. Large rounded wings show strong contrast between grey coverts and darker grey flight feathers. Juvenile dark-crowned but lacks black face-stripe; otherwise dull grey overall with a greyish bill. Distinctive form in flight, with neck and head retracted back towards body to create a bulge, and legs extending well beyond tail. Flight slow and ungainly. Call a harsh, loud, croaky *krrek*, often uttered when disturbed and in flight. Common and widespread resident.

PURPLE HERON *Ardea purpurea* 78–90cm

Large, slender heron with rich reddish-purple and grey plumage. Smaller than Grey Heron, with a narrow head, long neck and long, pointed yellow bill. Adult has reddish-brown sides to otherwise white head, neck and underparts, distinct black border from bill to lower breast, and long black streaking through breast. Upperparts dark grey with purple hue to wing-coverts. Juvenile less distinctive, with mottled brown plumage; white neck and breast finely streaked black, and head finely striped rufous brown. Long legs clearly extend from tail in flight and toes often spread; retracted neck more angled than in larger Grey. Call a short, croaky *krrek*. Nests colonially. Frequents shallow wetlands, reedbeds, lakes and rivers, open grasslands and marshes. Scarce, local summer visitor; fairly common passage migrant.

▼ *Adult*

▼ *Adult in flight*

EURASIAN BITTERN *Botaurus stellaris* 70–80cm

Large, stocky, rather hunched brown heron with a thick neck, short legs and a prominent bill. Adult has pale buff to golden-brown plumage with black mottling and bars throughout, darker and more pronounced along back. Head with black crown and moustachial stripe. Paler yellowish-brown underparts also mottled, but fainter and more striped. Strong bill and legs yellowish green. Juvenile similar, but crown and moustachial stripe duller brown. Song is a characteristic hollow, low boom, made by territorial male. Highly secretive, often skulking in favoured reedbed habitat; not often seen in flight apart from low over reedbeds when travelling to and fro to feed young. Fairly scarce, widespread winter visitor and passage migrant; rare recent breeder in north Greece.

BLACK STORK *Ciconia nigra* 95–100cm

Very large, full-bodied waterbird with a long neck and legs and a prominent bill. Adult has oily green-purple gloss to black head, neck, breast and back, contrasting with white belly. Bill is large, red and pointed, with a slight bow. Eye surround and legs also red. Juvenile lacks red; legs, bill and eye surround greenish grey, and plumage overall drab brown rather than glossy black. Nests in treetops within old coniferous forests near water and open grasslands. Found in wetlands during spring passage. Scarce local summer visitor and passage migrant.

WHITE STORK *Ciconia ciconia* 100–115cm

Very large, tall, full-bodied waterbird with a long neck, legs and bill, and distinctive pied plumage. All ages show long red legs and a long, powerful, pointed red bill. Unmistakable when seen on the ground and in the air, with white plumage and black flight feathers and rump. Loud bill clattering at nest during courtship. Breeds in loose colonies, and often found nesting on artificial structures. Favours open wet grasslands, floodplains and irrigated land. Quite tolerant of human activity. Widespread and locally common summer visitor and passage migrant throughout north and central Greece and a few Aegean islands.

EURASIAN SPOONBILL *Platalea leucorodia* 80–93cm

Large, robust yet dainty all-white waterbird, with a unique long spoon-shaped bill and long neck and legs. Summer breeding adult has a yellowish tinge to shoulders and short, square-ended crest plumes. Legs and bill black, the latter tipped yellow. Non-breeding adult all-white. Juvenile similar but with black tips to primaries evident in flight, grey legs and pinkish spatulate bill. Flies with characteristic fast wingbeats, and with legs extended and neck fully extended forward (unlike similar Great Egret). Colonial nester. Prefers coastal lowlands, open marshes, lagoons and river deltas with freshwater and saltwater access. Rare local resident and summer visitor to central and northern coastal Greece and Lesvos.

▼ *Adult*

▼ *Adult in flight*

▲ Adult   ▲ In flight

GLOSSY IBIS *Plegadis falcinellus* 55–65cm

At a distance, this unusual, elegant waterbird looks like a large black Eurasian Curlew, with its long, downcurved, sickle-shaped bill and proportionally short legs and narrow, long neck. Close views of breeding adult reveal an oily, dark reddish-purple and green gloss to uniform plumage, with only a small white area to bill base and variable dark pinkish-yellow bill and legs. Non-breeding adult and juvenile similar, but duller, browner and lacking gloss, and with fine white streaks around head and neck. Flies strongly with legs and neck fully extended, often in groups and line formations. Colonial nester. Prefers lowland wetlands, shallow lakes, rivers, estuaries and wet grasslands. Common and very widespread passage migrant; rare local summer visitor to northern Greece.

GREATER FLAMINGO *Phoenicopterus roseus* 125–145cm

Very tall, graceful, familiar bird. Unmistakable shape, with extremely long legs and neck, and a large, broad, uniquely bent bill. Adult coloration as striking as shape, with bubblegum-pink bill and legs, the former tipped black, and white plumage above and below, with crimson-pink wing-coverts and black flight feathers. In flight, black and pink wings obvious from above and below, and overall form shows extraordinary length from extended legs and neck. Juvenile dull brown with white underbelly, dark legs and grey bill. Call is a goose-like cackle. Highly gregarious. Prefers shallow coastal lagoons, saltpans and saline lakes. Fairly widespread, locally common non-breeding visitor, most numerous in winter.

◀ Adult
▼ Adults in flight

▲ Adult

▲ Adult in flight

EUROPEAN HONEY BUZZARD *Pernis apivorus* 52–60cm

Large raptor, not unlike Common Buzzard in structure but with longer, narrower wings and tail, and slender, longer neck often visibly projected forward. Variable plumages, with dark, pale and rufous morphs. Adult most often shows pale grey-brown head with yellow eyes and legs. Grey-brown above and white below, with dark trailing edge to wings and tail, and large mottled brown spots on neck, breast and flanks. Undertail and uppertail with two distinct bars, noticeable in flight (absent in Common). Elusive woodland species, favouring pine forests with adjacent open country. Widespread but scarce summer visitor and passage migrant.

BLACK KITE *Milvus migrans* 55–60cm

Similar to Red Kite but smaller, with grey-brown plumage, shorter wings and a shorter, less forked tail. Adult mid-brown above, with paler brown shoulders and dusky-brown underwing. Paler 'window' on underwing evident but not as conspicuous or well defined as in Red Kite. Juvenile has pale-tipped greater coverts on upperwings. Prefers lowland habitats, wetlands, farmland, woodland and areas around human activities. Often found in large groups, mixing with Red Kite in winter. Rare local resident; scarce winter visitor, increasing annually in north-east and centre; scarce passage migrant.

▼ Adult

▼ Adult in flight

▲ Adult   ▲ Adult in flight

RED KITE *Milvus milvus* 60–66cm

Fairly large, long-winged raptor, with a distinctive long, deeply forked tail. Upperparts striking rufous brown, darker on wings, with black central feather streaks throughout. Head pale grey with fine black streaks, underparts rufous brown, bill and legs yellow. Tail unmarked rufous orange above, pale buff below. Wings mainly blackish grey above, with rufous-brown back and shoulders. Underwing grey and black below with obvious light 'windows' on outer primaries. Aerobatic, twisting flight, often using tail as a rudder. Prefers open country and wetlands with nearby forests; also often around human habitation. Rare winter visitor and passage migrant; wintering numbers increasing annually, particularly in centre and north.

WHITE-TAILED EAGLE *Haliaeetus albicilla* 70–90cm

Very large raptor with long, broad wings, a wedge-shaped tail, long neck and very heavy bill, creating a distinctive silhouette in flight. Adult (after five years) mottled brown with pale tawny-brown head and neck, and pale fringes to dark upperpart feathers. Underparts darker and more uniform brown. Powerful yellow bill and yellow legs, the latter partly obscured by heavily feathered brown 'trousers'. Tail pure white above and below. Juvenile more uniformly dark brown and rufous, with black tips to feathering throughout. Tail dark brown, bill dark with pale whitish base. Breeds near and frequents large lakes, rivers and coasts in the north-east. Rare local resident; locally regular winter visitor.

▼ Adult
▶ Adult in flight

▲ Adult   ▲ Adult in flight

BEARDED VULTURE *Gypaetus barbatus* 100–115cm

Also known as Lammergeier. Impressive vulture of high mountains (500–4,000m). Enormous silhouette in flight, with very long, pointed wings and a long, broad, wedge-shaped tail. Underparts, neck and head yellowish orange-buff, contrasting with slate-grey back and tail. Striking face pattern, with trailing black wattle and face mask. Prefers rugged slopes and alpine habitats above the treeline, mainly foraging alone. Rarest vulture in Europe, once widespread but now extinct in many countries. Nearly extinct as a breeding bird in Greece, and now found only on Crete, where it is resident.

EYGPTIAN VULTURE *Neophron percnopterus* 60–70cm

Small pale vulture. Adult mainly off-white throughout with dark brown in tail and wings. Bare skin patch around face and legs yellow-orange, and rather long bill yellow-orange with a hooked black tip. In flight, underparts appear white with contrasting black flight feathers and wedged-shaped white tail. Juvenile dark brown with paler feather fringes through upperparts and face. Legs and bill pale grey, the latter with a black tip. Often solitary, hunting over open countryside and hilly terrains. Rare local summer visitor; scarce passage migrant. Breeds in north-east Greece, including a few pairs in Dadia National Park.

▼ Adult   ▼ Adult in flight

▲ Adult

▲ Adult in flight

GRIFFON VULTURE *Gyps fulvus* 95–105cm

Very large, small-headed vulture with broad wings and conspicuous long 'fingers' visible in flight. Adult distinctive, with a dark brown tail and flight feathers, pale sandy-brown body and wing-coverts, white neck, head and neck ruff, and bulbous yellowish bill. Underwing dark rufous brown with lighter patchy streaking and dark brown flight feathers and tail-band. Juvenile similar but duller brown above and bill grey. Fairly common but local resident, mainly in northern Greece, with small numbers spread across a few colonies; the highest concentration is in Crete.

CINEREOUS VULTURE *Aegypius monachus* 100–110cm

Also known as Black Vulture. One of the largest raptors in the world, more eagle-like in appearance, with long, broad wings. Dark chocolate brown throughout, underwing with almost black coverts contrasting with lighter flight feathers. Secondary tips very pointed, creating a 'toothed' appearance, primary tips deeply 'fingered.' Adult (after six years) has a pale buff neck ruff around head and down to breast, set against a bald whitish-buff crown and lores, and dark brown face, throat and neck-patch. Deep bill has a yellow base and dark bulbous tip. Juvenile dark brown throughout, including head and neck ruff, with pink bill base. Found in mountainous terrains and lowland forests with exposed rocky outcrops. Rare local resident. Through conservation efforts, one small breeding population exists in Dadia National Park.

▼ Juvenile and adult

▼ Adult in flight

SHORT-TOED SNAKE EAGLE *Circaetus gallicus* 62–67cm

Also known as Short-toed Eagle. Medium-sized robust raptor with long, broad wings, a short tail, large head and distinctive plumage (although beware juvenile Common Buzzard). In all ages, very pale with white underparts, contrasting with well-defined dark brown head and neck, and coarse brown barring to underwings. Three or four dark bars apparent on uppertail and undertail. Upperparts uniform, variable pale to dark brown. Legs and small bill grey, eyes yellow. Favours open hillsides, plains, meadows and forests. Often seen gliding on flat wings and hovering like a Common Kestrel. Fairly widespread, common summer visitor to mainland and islands.

WESTERN MARSH HARRIER *Circus aeruginosus* 48–56cm

Also known as Marsh Harrier. Large, narrow-winged harrier, the size of a Common Buzzard but with a slimmer head and body, long wings and tail, and notably long legs. Often flies with wings held in a distinct 'V'. Male strikingly tricoloured, with pale grey wings contrasting with chestnut back, shoulders and body, and black tips to primaries. Legs and bill base yellow. Female and juvenile plainer brown throughout, often with cream-buff crown, throat and shoulders. Bill dark on juvenile. Prefers open wetlands, reedbeds and agricultural habitats. Fairly scarce, declining resident, mainly in north mainland; common, widespread winter visitor and passage migrant, more numerous in spring.

▼ *Adult male*

▼ *Adult female*

▲ *Adult male in flight*
◀ *Adult male (top), Adult female (below)*

HEN HARRIER *Circus cyaneus* 44–52cm

Smaller than Marsh Harrier, rather stocky, and with long, broad wings and a long tail. Male has pale grey head and upperparts, white rump, clear-cut white underparts and a large black primary-tip patch, evident from above and below. In flight, shows five wing-tip 'fingers' and dark trailing edge to underwing. Eyes, bill base and legs bright yellow. Female and juvenile have brown upperparts, pale facial disc and broadly banded tail. Underparts warm brown and white, with variable brown streaking and dark-barred wings, as in female Montagu's Harrier. Juvenile underparts warm buff and heavily streaked, unlike juvenile Montagu's and Pallid harriers. Favours variable flat, open countryside on passage, and wetlands, marshes, reedbeds and agricultural land in winter. Widespread, locally common winter visitor; scarcer passage migrant.

PALLID HARRIER *Circus macrourus* 40–48cm

Male pale grey above and white below, with black wing-tips. Superficially similar to male Hen and Montagu's Harriers, but much paler grey above and more extensively white below, including throat, and has narrow wedge-shaped black wing-tip patch. Female and juvenile brown above, with white rump and broad-banded tail. Female has dusky-brown inner secondaries above and below, and underwing-coverts more speckled chestnut and darker than in female Hen or Montagu's. Wing shape and number of primary 'fingers' (four) best features to separate it from similar female Hen. Juvenile has uniform chestnut underparts with obvious buff-white collar, and pale tips to inner primaries (black in Montagu's). Wide-spread but scarce passage migrant throughout, most common in spring.

▼ *Adult female in flight*

▼ *Adult male*

▲ Adult male   ▲ Adult female

MONTAGU'S HARRIER *Circus pygargus* 43–47cm

Slender, with a long tail and wings, and a buoyant 'tern'-like flight. Male grey above with white rump-patch and sizeable black wing-tip patch, like Hen Harrier, but in flight shows four primary 'fingers' on wing-tips and prominent black bar across secondaries. Head and upper breast grey, underwing-coverts barred chestnut and belly white with fine chestnut streaks. Female lacks dusky inner secondaries of female Pallid Harrier, chestnut underwing-coverts barred (not mottled) and pale collar often visible. Very like female Hen, but separable on structure and primary 'fingers'. Juvenile resembles Pallid, with chestnut underparts and underwing-coverts, but lacks pale collar and primary tips are all dark. Found in open countryside, marshes, wetlands and farmland. Rare local summer visitor to far north; fairly common, widespread passage migrant.

NORTHERN GOSHAWK *Accipiter gentilis* 48–62cm

Large, strong accipiter, with broad wings and a long, broadly banded tail. Female substantially larger than male. Male may be confused with female Eurasian Sparrowhawk, but much larger, heavier, rounder-tailed and broader-winged. Adult slate grey above and white with dark barring below. Supercilium straight and striking white, ear-coverts dark and eyes orange. Juvenile brown above, and warm buff below with dark vertical streaking. Very elusive. Often hunts low, gliding over forests. In early spring performs 'sky dance' display flight. Fairly common and widespread resident, mainly in northern and central Greece and on some larger islands.

◀ Adult
▼ Adult in flight

▲ Adult female   ▲ Adult male

EURASIAN SPARROWHAWK *Accipiter nisus* 28–38cm

Small raptor with rounded wings and long square-ended tail. Male has slate-grey head and upperparts, with variable small white patches. Underparts white from throat to undertail, with orange-brown wash to cheek and throat and orange-brown barring to breast. Eyes and legs yellow. Female grey and white; resembles small Northern Goshawk, but smaller and with slighter build. Juvenile dark brown above, with dark bars across white underparts, these broken and more heart-shaped on upper breast and throat. Fast, agile hunter. Favours forests for breeding but also occurs in urban areas, gardens, parks and farmland. Fairly widespread and locally a reasonably common resident; common and widespread winter visitor; passage migrant. More numerous in north and centre.

LEVANT SPARROWHAWK *Accipiter brevipes* 32–38cm

Small falcon-like raptor, with narrow, pointed wings and a slightly shorter tail than Eurasian Sparrowhawk. Sexes similar sizes. Male has grey-blue upperparts with black wing-tips, broken uppertail bands, grey-blue cheek and dark eyes. Underparts white with pale orange-brown breast barring. In flight, white underwing looks unmarked but for diagnostic black wing-tips. Female grey-brown above and white below with dense brown barring across breast and conspicuous brown central throat line at close range. Underwing finely barred, wing-tips black. Juvenile like juvenile Eurasian Sparrowhawk but with streaky (not barred) breast. Prefers lowlands, open woodland and forested valleys. Fairly widespread, locally a reasonably common summer visitor; passage migrant. Commonest in north and on larger Aegean islands.

▼ Adult female   ▼ Adult male

▲ Adult   ▲ Adult in flight

COMMON BUZZARD *Buteo buteo* 51–57cm

Large, compact raptor with a rounded head, broad wings and short tail.
Plumage highly variable, mainly mid-brown above with white and brown
underparts. Mottled brown underwing-coverts, dark carpal patches on
underwing, and obvious dark trailing edge along wings and tail. Mottled
brown body often shows paler belly crescent. Bill and legs yellow. Call an
eagle-like *piiyay*. Commonly seen soaring low over woodland and
perched in trees, on posts or on telegraph wires. Favours open
countryside, farmland with trees, forests and even large wetlands in
winter. Common and widespread resident; winter visitor throughout.
Rufous-toned eastern subspecies, Steppe Buzzard (*B. b. vulpinus*), also
occurs in the north.

LONG-LEGGED BUZZARD *Buteo rufinus* 50–65cm

More robust than similar rare Rough-legged Buzzard (*B. lagopus*; not
illustrated), and larger and longer-winged than Steppe Buzzard
(*B. b. vulpinus*; see Common Buzzard). Highly variable colour forms, but
distinct orange hues to plumage, orange-red tail, pale head and
whitish underparts are common features. Often distinct black carpal
patches and dark trailing edge to wings, and commonly lacks trailing
black tail-band. Prefers dry, open habitats; nests in woodlands. Fairly
widespread but scarce resident; locally scarce partial migrant and
winter visitor, when influxes to north boost numbers. Commoner in
south and on larger islands.

▲ Adult

▲ Adult in flight

LESSER SPOTTED EAGLE *Aquila pomarina* 60–65cm

Compact, broad-winged brown eagle, with a paler head, neck and upperwing-coverts. Underparts show brown body and head contrasting with almost black flight feathers and tail. Head and bill small for an eagle. Adult shows clear white primary patch on upperwing and distinct white 'U' on rump. Juvenile darker brown, with small rufous nape-patch, white tips to wing and tail feathers (obvious at rest and in flight), and a diffuse white primary patch on upperparts. Call a high-pitched bark. Soars and glides with arched, drooping wing silhouette and prominent wing-tip 'fingers'. Breeds in wooded areas adjacent to open countryside. Fairly widespread, locally common summer visitor and passage migrant. Overwintering records increasing.

GREATER SPOTTED EAGLE *Aquila clanga* 65–72cm

Resembles Lesser Spotted Eagle, but bulkier, darker brown, and with broader wings and longer primary wing-tip 'fingers'. Adult chocolate brown throughout, with darker head and coverts contrasting with paler flight feathers. Lacks the paler head and upperwing-coverts of Lesser and has less defined white upper primary patch, if any. Juvenile easier to identify, nearly brown-black with usually numerous white spots on upperwing forming rows along wing-coverts, clear white 'U' on rump and white tail-tips. Call a loud, low-pitched bark. Primarily a forest species. Scarce local winter visitor; numbers can build up in larger northern marshes, particularly in severe winters.

EASTERN IMPERIAL EAGLE *Aquila heliaca* 72–83cm

Large, heavy eagle with long, broad wings, a square tail, and a large bill and head. Adult dark brown, with a golden-brown head and nape, and white shoulder. Underwing grey with almost black underwing-coverts. Tail grey with a broad black band at tip. Juvenile pale, sandy buff above with many white spots to tips of grey-brown wing feathers. In flight, sandy-buff underparts and underwing-coverts contrast with dark flight feathers and tail. Pale 'window' to inner three primaries. Similar above, but white spots in wings form obvious narrow wing-bars, primary 'window' still evident and rump buff-white. Subadult very variable. Prefers forests and open plains. Rare passage migrant; uncommon local winter visitor (mainly juveniles) to Evros Delta and larger north and west wetlands.

GOLDEN EAGLE *Aquila chrysaetos* 75–88cm

Very large, powerful eagle, with a long tail and wings. Bill and legs yellow. Conspicuous pale yellow-brown to light rufous-brown crown and nape in all ages. Adult grey above with black bands through flight feathers. Tail grey with dark bars and broad black tip. Wing-coverts worn, bleached-looking, showing variable pale panel. In flight, underparts two-toned, with golden-brown body and underwing-coverts contrasting with pale grey flight feathers. Juvenile and subadult variable, browner throughout, with large white patches on upper and underwing and broad, black-tipped white tail. Often seen soaring high on thermals. Widespread, locally uncommon, declining resident in mountainous regions on mainland and in Crete.

▲ *Pale morph adult*   ▲ *Dark morph adult*

BOOTED EAGLE *Aquila pennata* 45–53cm

Similar size to Common Buzzard, with longer, sharp-edged tail and narrower wings with longer primary-tip 'fingers'. Pale and dark morphs, all brown above when perched, with rather bleached upperwing and dark flight feathers. Pale adult shows whitish underparts. In flight, underparts and underwing-coverts whitish, contrasting with blackish flight feathers. Darker morphs show uniform brown underparts and underwing-coverts, the latter with a black bar adjacent to greyish flight feathers. All have pale inner primary panels, pale brown tail from above, bleached upperwing patches and small white foreneck patches, like 'landing lights' when seen head on in flight. Prefers open countryside; breeds in woodlands. Fairly widespread, uncommon summer visitor and passage migrant. Low numbers breed in northern Greece.

BONELLI'S EAGLE *Aquila fasciata* 65–72cm

Robust, medium-sized eagle with protruding head and long tail. In flight, adult underparts and leading-edge coverts white with dark flecks, and flight feathers diffused light grey, contrasting with angled black underwing-covert bars. Tail grey with broad black band at tip. Upperparts greyish, often with whitish mantle patch. Juvenile brown above, warm buff below. In flight, warm buff underparts and underwing-coverts contrast with lightly barred grey flight feathers and tail. Primary tips and small carpal-bar black. Uncommon light morph juvenile shows white and pale grey underparts with black wing-tips. Frequents forests and mountainous habitats. Nests in rocky gorges near the sea. Rare resident, more common in south-west coastal mainland and islands, with the highest density in Crete.

▼ *Adult*   ▼ *Adult in flight*

▲ Adult

▲ Adult in flight

OSPREY *Pandion haliaetus* 55–58cm

Easily distinguished from other medium to large raptors by plumage. Upperparts chocolate brown; wings long, narrowing to four-'fingered' primary tips. Underparts and head white, the latter with dark brown mask, yellow eyes and diffuse brown necklace. In flight, underwing flight feathers and tail chequered brown and white, with darker brown carpal patches and black bar separating flight feathers from white underwing-coverts. Juvenile has pale feather fringes to dark brown upperparts. Favours coasts and large wetlands. Hovers and plummets into water to grab fish prey with talons. Widespread but scarce passage migrant to Greece; occasionally overwinters.

LESSER KESTREL *Falco naumanni* 29–32cm

Small, dainty falcon with a long, narrow tail. Protruding central tail feathers a key feature in flight. Male similar to Common Kestrel but with grey-blue crown and nape, and plain chestnut back separated from blackish flight feathers on upperwing by blue-grey panel. Uppertail and rump pale grey with black band. Body buff with sparse dark spots, and underwings with cleaner white flight feathers than Common. Female and juvenile hard to distinguish from Common aside from tail projection, but paler throughout, with finer spotting to buff breast. Colonial nester in derelict buildings, towers and roof spaces in villages and towns, less commonly in natural sites. Migrates in groups, often resting on telegraph cables or isolated trees. Declining but widespread, uncommon summer visitor and passage migrant.

▼ Adult male

▼ Adult female

▲ Adult male

▲ Adult female

COMMON KESTREL *Falco tinnunculus* 32–35cm

Similar to Lesser Kestrel but marginally larger and lacks projecting central tail feathers. Male has dark-streaked grey head and moustachial stripe. Upperparts chestnut brown and underparts warm buff, both with dark spotting throughout. In flight, upperparts tricoloured, with chestnut back and inner wing, black flight feathers and greater coverts, and pale grey rump and black-tipped tail. Female and juvenile have a light brown crown, and coppery-brown upperparts and buff-white underparts with dense black spotting. In flight, they resemble male but with barring through greyish tail. Often seen hovering above open habitats, before dropping onto prey. Common and widespread resident; numbers increase in winter as birds arrive from further north.

RED-FOOTED FALCON *Falco vespertinus* 29–31cm

Small, elegant falcon. Male unmistakable, with slate-grey plumage throughout, brick-red 'trousers' and undertail-coverts, and red legs, bill base and eye-ring. In flight, upperparts grey with lighter grey patches on primaries. Female orange-buff and lightly streaked below, and blue-grey above with dense black barring. Head orange-buff with whitish face and dark eye-mask and moustachial stripe. Legs and bill base orange. Juvenile has whitish underparts with dark streaks and brownish-grey barred upperparts; face pale with dark eye-mask and crown pale brown. Similar to juvenile Hobby, but with good views separable on dark-barred uppertail (solid grey in Hobby). Migrates in loose flocks, often perching together on telegraph wires and sparse trees around open cultivation. Common passage migrant throughout, particularly in spring.

▼ Adult female

▼ Adult male in flight

▲ Adult male ▲ Adult female

MERLIN *Falco columbarius* 25–30cm

Small, compact falcon. Fast and agile, often seen fleetingly while hunting low with rapid wingbeats and glides in pursuit of prey. Male grey-blue above and orange-buff below and around collar, with fine black streaking throughout. In flight, shows grey-blue upperparts, darker outer wing, and narrow grey tail with broad black band at tip. Crown grey-blue with finely streaked whitish face and poorly defined moustachial stripe. Female and juvenile dull grey-brown above; underparts buff-white with dark streaking on breast, heavier along flanks. Crown brown; face whitish, finely streaked, with dark moustachial stripe. Dark tail with white bars, notable from above and below. Prefers open lowland, but also noted in mountains. Widespread but scarce winter visitor, mainly to north.

EURASIAN HOBBY *Falco subbuteo* 30–36cm

Similar in size to Common Kestrel, but with a shorter tail, almost swift-like shape and long, pointed wings. Very fast aerial hunter like Merlin. Adult has slate-grey upperparts and whitish underparts with black streaking. Whitish throat and cheeks contrast with distinctive black facial mask and moustachial stripe. Brick-red 'trousers' and vent diagnostic. Juvenile browner above, with cream (not whitish) underparts and no red 'trousers'. Similar to Juvenile Red-footed Falcon but duskier (see that species). Fairly widespread passage migrant; scarcer summer visitor. More common in centre and north.

▼ Adult ▼ Adult in flight

▲ *Adult pale morph*

▲ *Adult in flight*

ELEONORA'S FALCON *Falco eleonorae* 36–40cm

Rather large, long-tailed, long-winged falcon. Pale and dark morphs occur, the former commoner and not dissimilar to Hobby, although overall size and facial pattern differ and birds lack red 'trousers' or vent. Adult pale morph dark brown above and rufous brown with dark streaking below. Crown and moustachial stripe brown, cheeks rounded and white. Dark morph uniformly dark brown throughout. In flight, both morphs have dark underwing-coverts contrasting with lighter flight feathers. Juvenile a duskier-buff version of pale adult, with pale brown edges to dull grey upperpart feathers. Breeds on offshore islands, nests on rocky cliffs and in crevices. Fairly widespread but scarce summer visitor, noted widely across mainland during spring arrival; some overwintering in recent years.

51

PEREGRINE FALCON *Falco peregrinus* 36–48cm

Powerful, compact falcon. Adult slate grey above with black-barred white underparts, dark grey crown and broad moustachial stripe against white cheek and throat. Feet and eye-ring yellow. Underwing white with fine dark barring. Juvenile darker brown above, with denser brown streaking to buff-cream underparts and browner underwing-coverts visible in flight. Resident birds belong to the race *F. p. brookei* (may show rufous on nape), while many wintering birds are the nominate race *F. p. peregrinus*. Widespread but scarce resident of mountains and coasts; fairly uncommon winter visitor.

▼ *Adult*

▼ *Adult in flight*

WATER RAIL *Rallus aquaticus* 23–28cm

Shy, slender-bodied rail with a slightly curved red bill, long pinkish legs and a long neck. Tail often held cocked, giving a distinctive appearance. Adult warm brown above with black centres to feathers, contrasting with grey underparts and heavy black-and-white barring on flanks. Juvenile similar but duller and lacks grey underparts. Call like a pig's squeal. Prefers freshwater margins, reedbeds, ditches and muddy ground. Often elusive, walking among dense aquatic vegetation. Common and widespread resident and passage migrant. Numbers often increase dramatically in harsh winters as birds filter south.

SPOTTED CRAKE *Porzana porzana* 22–24cm

Overall shape and disposition similar to that of Water Rail, but smaller, with a rounder, more compact body, longer wings, greenish legs and a short bill. All ages brown, with black centres to feathers on upperparts and more restricted grey on underparts than Water Rail; characteristic fine white spotting and barring throughout. Adult has stout yellowish bill with red base, black to front of face and pale buff undertail, obvious when cocked. Juvenile has duller to head and bill. Frequents lowland wetlands and freshwater margins. Widespread but scarce passage migrant, more common in spring; winter visitor.

LITTLE CRAKE *Porzana parva* 18–20cm

Small, slender crake with a long primary projection. Male similar to Water Rail and Baillon's Crake at a distance, but dull brown upperparts only lightly marked white, underparts and face plain grey, bill yellow-green with red base, and flanks unbarred (see Baillon's). Undertail black with many white bars. Female upperparts, bill and undertail similar, but underparts very pale buff to white, and grey on face restricted. Juvenile resembles female, but more extensive white underparts with flank barring. Favours freshwater wetlands and marshy fringes. Breeds in reedbeds. Rare local summer visitor; fairly common passage migrant.

BAILLON'S CRAKE *Porzana pusilla* 17–19cm

Small, dumpy crake, similar to male Little Crake and Water Rail on plumage, but tiny, with short primary projection and tail. Sexes similar, distinguished from Little by lack of red on bill base and richer brown upperparts with denser white markings on back. Immature similar but underparts extensively barred. Prefers shallow, sedge-rich wetlands and freshwater margins on passage. Breeding within Greece largely unknown. Fairly widespread but rare passage migrant, more common in spring.

CORN CRAKE *Crex crex* 27–30cm

Larger than Water Rail, more like an oversized partridge. Very skulking, land-based bird, rarely seen in the open; more likely heard. Very distinctive plumage, with chestnut wings, black-centred brown upperpart feathers, and greyish face and underparts. White and brown barring evident along flanks. Legs long and pinkish, feet hang down in flight, and bill short and pinkish. Song a repeated *crex-crex*. Widespread but rare passage migrant throughout. Has declined due to hunting, habitat loss and changes in farming practices across Europe.

COMMON MOORHEN *Gallinula chloropus* 32–35cm

Adult plumage distinctive, almost black with brown and blue hues, broken white line along flanks and white undertail. Bill red with yellow tip and extended red shield, legs long and yellow-green. Juvenile dull brown with whitish underparts. Often seen swimming with jerking head motion, replaced by jerky tail motion on land. Found in a variety of freshwater wetlands, from small ponds and marshes to larger lakes, rivers and, often, urban areas. Common and widespread resident throughout lowlands, numbers increasing in winter with arrivals from north.

EURASIAN COOT *Fulica atra* 36–38cm

Round-headed, round-bodied, plump waterbird, slightly larger than Common Moorhen. Very distinctive, dark grey to sooty-black plumage contrasting with white bill and bill shield and red eye. Legs long, robust and yellow-grey, feet long with extended flat lobes. Juvenile brown-grey with paler whitish underparts; lacks white bill and shield. Frequents a variety of freshwater habitats, from lakes, ponds, rivers and reservoirs, to urban areas, canals and ditches; also found in estuarine habitats, particularly in winter. Often seen swimming alone or in winter flocks. Can be very vocal. Common and widespread resident; very common winter visitor.

COMMON CRANE *Grus grus* 110–120cm

Very large, elegant wading bird with long legs and neck, small head and oval-shaped body ending in a ruffle of extended 'tail' feathers (actually tertials). Adult grey with black-and-white neck and head, and red patch on crown. Bill fairly long and pale bone/yellow, eye red. Huge, stiff-winged form in flight (not unlike a stork or vulture), with head and legs extended, and black flight feathers contrasting with pale grey wings and body. Juvenile paler grey and plain throughout. Irregular passage migrant, most often seen in spring. Most sightings are of small flocks in coastal wetland and marsh habitats from the north-east, south to Crete and the south-east Aegean Islands.

◀ *Adult male (centre) and females*
▼ *Adult in flight*

BLACK-WINGED STILT *Himantopus himantopus* 35–40cm

Unmistakable dainty black-and-white wader with very long bubblegum-pink legs, a long neck and a needle-thin black bill. Adult has variable black on crown, ear-coverts, nape and back, and all-black wings. Underparts white (head whiter on female), with pink flush to breast in summer male. Juvenile similar, but upperparts and crown dusky brown and scaly, and legs darkish yellow. Tail and rump white in all ages, obvious in flight. Flight fast, with rapidly flicking wings, and with legs trailing behind body and neck and head extending forward. Frequents saltwater, freshwater and brackish wetlands throughout. Common summer visitor and passage migrant.

EURASIAN OYSTERCATCHER *Haematopus ostralegus* 40–45cm

Unmistakable large wader with black upperparts and white underparts, pink legs and a long, straight, carrot-like orange bill. Eyes red with bright orange eye-ring. Obvious white band across black upper wings and V-shaped white rump in flight. Juvenile still pied but appears dirtier, with duller, dark-tipped bill and grey legs. Very scarce and localised resident; fairly common winter visitor, with large influxes from the north, often in flocks, arriving along coasts. Prefers rocky coastal areas and shorelines. Once a more common breeder, now confined to a few small breeding populations in coastal wetlands in the north.

▼ *Adult*

▼ *Adult in flight*

PIED AVOCET *Recurvirostra avosetta* 42–45cm

Delicate wader with long grey legs, an upcurved black bill, and snow-white and jet-black plumage. Black on crown and nape, with large black patches on greater coverts and primaries, obvious in flight. Juvenile similar, but black replaced with brown and white not as pure. Feeds by sweeping bill from side to side in shallow waters. Prefers mudflats, shallow pools, estuaries and marshes, both brackish and saltwater. Fairly widespread and locally fairly common resident; common winter visitor. Only a few fragmented breeding colonies now exist, mainly in northern coastal wetlands.

EURASIAN STONE-CURLEW *Burhinus oedicnemus* 40–44cm

An unusual-looking robust wader with a large head and long wings, like a large plover. Stout bill yellow with a black tip; large, bulbous eye and long legs yellow. Pale sandy-brown plumage with dark streaking to upperparts. White belly and white underwing with black trailing edge. Strong white stripe above and below eye, dark-edged white wing-bar (obvious in standing birds). In flight, note striking black-and-white upperwing patches. Often motionless by day, vocal and active from dusk to dawn. Strangely shy of water, preferring drier margins, arid habitats, grassland and bare stony ground neighbouring coastal wetlands. Fairly widespread and locally common summer visitor and passage migrant. Breeds mainly on north and west mainland coasts and some Aegean islands. Numbers peak during spring and autumn migrations.

COLLARED PRATINCOLE *Glareola pratincola* 24–28cm

Unusual medium-sized wader. Long wings and forked tail give it a tern-like appearance in flight, and stance and plumage make it appear plover-like at rest. Adult upperparts, head and breast smoky brown, belly white and lower breast yellow. Throat cream, bordered black. Bill small and stout, with a bright red base and black tip. Eye large and black with white eye-stripe below. In flight, white rump and dark brown wedge to primaries contrast with soft brown upperparts. White trailing edge to inner wing and dark chestnut underwing-coverts separate it from Black-winged Pratincole (see that species below). Juvenile dusky grey-brown and heavily scaled above, with a spotted dusky breast-band. Found on dry and wet, flat, open terrain with sparse low vegetation. Scarce local summer visitor; widespread passage migrant, more numerous in spring. Breeds in small numbers throughout northern wetlands.

BLACK-WINGED PRATINCOLE *Glareola nordmanni* 24–28cm

Very similar to Collared Pratincole but separable with care. Upperparts smoky grey-brown, upperwing dark brown and lacks white trailing edge to secondaries, contrast between coverts and dark primary wedge negligible, and underwing-coverts black. Close inspection also reveals less red at bill base and more extensive black area around lores. Juvenile like juvenile Collared but underwing-coverts black, not chestnut. Favours flat wet meadows and marshy habitats. Rare yet widespread passage migrant throughout.

LITTLE RINGED PLOVER *Charadrius dubius* 14–15cm
....
Small, delicate plover, less rounded than Common Ringed Plover and with a slightly slimmer, longer, all-dark bill. Plumage similar, but summer adult shows characteristic yellow eye-ring, white band across crown bordering black forehead-band, and pinkish (not orange) legs. In flight, lacks white wing-bar. Winter adult retains a reduced yellow eye-ring, black plumage becomes brown and buff around head, and legs are pinkish grey. Juvenile similar to winter adult, but duller brown with some pale fringes to upperparts and a buff supercilium. More shy than Common Ringed. Prefers freshwater margins, inland mountain river valleys and lakes in open terrain. Fairly common, widespread summer visitor and passage migrant.

COMMON RINGED PLOVER *Charadrius hiaticula* 18–20cm
....
Robust, rotund plover, slightly larger than Little Ringed Plover and Kentish Plover. Summer adult upperparts greyish brown, underparts white. Head black and white, and breast-band complete and black. Legs short and orange, and stout bill yellow with a black tip. In flight, shows white wing-bar and dark central tail bordered white. In winter adult, black plumage is replaced by brown and bill darkens. Juvenile similar to winter adult but with pale fringes to dull brown upperparts, creating a scalloped effect. Frequents coastal habitats, sandy and shingle beaches, and tidal zones. Fairly common, widespread passage migrant, more frequent in autumn; rare winter visitor.

▼ *Adult summer*   ▼ *Juvenile*

 ▲ *Adult male*　　　　　　　　▲ *Adult female*

KENTISH PLOVER *Charadrius alexandrinus* 15–17cm

Small, compact plover with a slight build. Confusion possible with Little Ringed and Common Ringed plovers, but patterning paler and more refined, and legs longer. Proportionally large head-to-body ratio, and short primary projection and blunt rear give squat appearance. All ages have pale sandy-brown to grey upperparts and white underparts. Summer male has black legs; lacks black markings of Little Ringed and Common Ringed, and instead has broken black breast-band, black eye-stripe, white supercilium, small black bar on forehead and subtle but diagnostic rufous patch on nape. Female and winter male duller brown-grey above, with pale brown head markings and very diffuse, broken dark breast-band. Juvenile even paler above, with no discernible dark areas to upperparts or head. Common and widespread resident of coastal wetlands.

EUROPEAN GOLDEN PLOVER *Pluvialis apricaria* 26–29cm

Bulky-bodied medium-sized plover. Smaller than Grey Plover, with fairly short dark legs, small rounded head, small dark bill and beady black eyes. On the ground, often holds an upright stance, with short walks and quick pecks after food. Summer plumage very distinctive, but few birds reaching Greece will retain the characteristic white-bordered black underparts, breast and facial patterning. Instead, all ages in winter show densely speckled golden-brown and black upperparts and white underparts, with a streaked and speckled golden-brown chest, neck and crown. Frequents farmland, short open grassland and saltmarsh fringes, mainly in north and west mainland. Often in large flocks, and with Northern Lapwing. Fairly common winter visitor.

▼ *Adult summer*　　　　　　　▼ *Adult winter*

▲ Adult winter

GREY PLOVER *Pluvialis squatarola* 27–30cm

Similar to European Golden Plover, but head and body stockier, bill larger
and posture more hunched. Summer adult has boldly speckled black-and-
grey upperparts; jet-black face, breast and underbelly contrast with white
supercilium and neck-stripe. In winter, all ages have mottled grey-and-black
upperparts with some buff tones, cleaner underparts with white below, and
fine buff-grey speckling and streaking to breast. Note diagnostic black
armpits in flight (white in European Golden). Frequents all major coastal
wetlands; less common on islands. Occurs on coastal mudflats and shallow
sandy coastal bays in winter (European Golden prefers drier arable habitats).
Fairly widespread and locally common winter visitor and passage migrant
(summer-plumaged birds often seen in spring in the north).

SPUR-WINGED LAPWING *Vanellus spinosus* 25–27cm

Distinctly pied wader, with an upright stance, long dark legs and
rounded wings. Adult has black crown, throat-stripe, breast and tail,
contrasting with pale brown wings and white cheek-patch, neck and
underparts. Juvenile not as clean-looking, with pale fringes to brown
back and brownish crown. Prefers dry, open coastal margins. First
recorded as a rare breeding species in northern Greece in 1960, with
estimates of up to 70 pairs found in the late 1960s; now reduced to a
handful of sites, mainly around Nestos and Evros deltas. Rare local
summer visitor; scarce passage migrant, more regularly seen in spring,
particularly on southern Aegean islands.

▲ Adult summer
▶ In flight (top), Adult winter (below)

NORTHERN LAPWING
Vanellus vanellus 28–31cm

Pigeon-sized black-and-white wader with long, thin crest plumes. Upperparts dark, with a green-purple gloss in good light. Summer male has a black forehead, face, cheek-stripe and breast-band. Summer female and juvenile similar, but have a shorter crest, broken white areas on face and breast, and solid white throat. In winter, all birds have pale scalloping on dark upperparts. In all plumages, supercilium, cheek and underparts pure white, undertail-coverts chestnut orange. Legs dark pink, bill dark. In flight, wings appear strikingly large and rounded, and underwing extensively black with white at base. Frequents coastal saltmarshes, pastures and open country; often seen in characteristic tumbling, rolling display flight in spring. Scarce local resident in the north, breeding primarily in Evros Delta; otherwise common and widespread winter visitor throughout.

SANDERLING *Calidris alba* 20–21cm

Resembles Dunlin in size, but with a shorter, straighter black bill. Notably larger than Little Stint, another confusion species. Summer adult shows red-brown tones and dark spotting to head, neck and upper breast, and variable amounts of pale-fringed chestnut-and-black feathers on upperparts. In flight, upperwing has wide white wing-bar, bordered black (wider than in Dunlin). At close range, note lack of hind toe. Winter adult plainer, silvery grey above and white below. Juvenile has neat black-and-white spangled upperparts and pure white underparts. Favours sandy beaches, characteristically running along the tideline. Fairly common, widespread passage migrant on mainland (especially north-east and west) and larger islands; scarce winter visitor.

▼ Juvenile

▼ Adult spring

▲ *Adult spring*

LITTLE STINT *Calidris minuta* 12–14cm

Tiny, compact sandpiper, with a short black bill and black legs. Summer adult has warm red-brown upperparts (brightest in males), with striking black centres and rich chestnut or white fringes to feathers. Head and breast brownish with fine blackish streaks. Underparts clean white. Winter adult much colder and plainer, with grey upperparts, feathers with fine black centres and white fringes, and white underparts. Juvenile more reminiscent of summer adult, warm brown above but with striking white 'tramlines' along back. Occurs in both saline and freshwater habitats, favouring shallow coastal lagoons, saltpans, beaches, mudflats and small pools. Common and widespread passage migrant throughout; common winter visitor.

TEMMINCK'S STINT *Calidris temminckii* 13–15cm

Size of Little Stint, but with a longer body, tail and wings. Legs shorter and yellowish, and dark bill slightly downcurved. Summer adult has mottled brown and grey upperparts, with white-tipped, dark-centred feathers. Head and upper breast mottled brown-grey, clearly demarcated from white lower breast and belly, like a tiny Common Sandpiper. Upperparts greyer in winter adult and plainer brown in juvenile. In flight, note restricted white wing-bar, obvious white outer-tail feathers and dark central tail-stripe. More retiring than Little Stint, favouring vegetated margins of freshwater pools, lakes and rivers, and marshes and saltpans. Fairly uncommon and widespread passage migrant, most numerous in spring.

▼ *Adult spring*

▲ Adult summer   ▲ Juvenile

CURLEW SANDPIPER *Calidris ferruginea* 18–19cm

Confusion with Dunlin possible, but slightly larger and more elegant, with longer legs and a longer, more downcurved bill. Summer adult shows mottled grey upperparts and rusty underparts, these almost solid brick red in male at height of summer and flecked white in female and late-summer male. Winter adult (not often seen) plainer, dark grey above and white below. Juvenile has strong supercilium and scaly plumage above, feathers with pale brown to black centres and pale fringes. Underparts white, and breast and head with peachy-buff tones and diffuse dark streaking. In flight, all birds show white rump. Occurs in coastal wetlands. Widespread and locally common passage migrant, sometimes very numerous in spring.

DUNLIN *Calidris alpina* 16–20cm

Small, short-necked, short-legged wader with a rather dumpy, rotund body. Overall size, bill length and bill curvature may vary. Summer adult has warm brown upperparts with white-edged black-and-chestnut feathers and a diagnostic black belly-patch. Crown chestnut, and face and chest white, all with dense dark streaking. Supercilium pale, and flanks and undertail white. Winter adult very different, with plain grey upperparts and white underparts (see Sanderling, Little Stint and Curlew Sandpiper). Juvenile similar, but browner above and with extensive dark streaking to underparts. In flight, shows white wing-bar and white outer-tail feathers, black central tail-stripe and blackish rump. Found on coastal mudflats, deltas, lagoons and saltpans. Common and very widespread winter visitor and passage migrant.

▼ Adult summer   ▼ Adult winter

BROAD-BILLED SANDPIPER *Calidris falcinellus* 16–17cm

Slightly smaller than Dunlin, with shorter legs and a subtly longer, deeper bill that curves downwards only near tip. Summer adult and juvenile show strong contrast between very dark upperparts and white underparts, not seen in other waders. Summer adult has extensive, almost black plumage to upperparts, broken by neat white or chestnut edging to feathers. Head boldly striped, with dark eye-stripe, obvious pale supercilium and thin whitish stripes each side of dark crown. Breast and flanks with numerous heavy streaks, which in full summer plumage form a complete breast-band. Winter adult more Dunlin-like, but differs in white edging to feathers on upperparts and pale head markings. Found on coastal wetlands. Widespread but scarce passage migrant.

RUFF *Calidris pugnax* 26–30cm

Large wader with a small head and bill, elongated body and long legs. Male is the size of Redshank, smaller female often only slightly larger than Dunlin. In breeding plumage (rare in Greece) male displays colourful feathered ruff and ear-tufts. Adult has orange legs, plain white to grey underparts, scalloped upperparts, and dark brown feathers edged brown-buff on back and wings, these becoming finer along mantle, back of neck and crown. In winter adult, bill black with orange along first third. Face plain brownish buff, often with a white bill base and white around eye. Juvenile apricot buff, warmer than grey-toned adult. Frequents freshwater and saline habitats throughout. Common and widespread passage migrant, particularly in spring; scarce winter visitor.

▼ *Juvenile*   ▼ *Adult (non-breeding)*

JACK SNIPE *Lymnocryptes minimus* 17–19cm

Small, compact, very secretive wader, only two-thirds the size of Common Snipe, and with a much shorter, deep-based bill. Legs rather short, yellowish. Densely patterned, cryptic plumage throughout, from chestnut brown to chocolate brown, buff and cream. Upperparts dark, with two pale golden 'tramlines' along back. Dark eye-stripe, cheek crescent and crown contrast with pale cream split supercilium. Often crouched and hidden, making silent short, low escape flight when flushed (see Common). Often feeds with characteristic rhythmic 'body-bobbing'. Prefers wet margins of marshland and grassland, ditches and flooded arable land. Scarce passage migrant and winter visitor.

COMMON SNIPE *Gallinago gallinago* 25–27cm

Dumpy, heavily patterned cryptic wader with a very long, straight bill and short yellow-grey legs. Plumage in all ages boldly striped brown, black, cream and buff. Dark brown eye-stripe and crown, and pale buff supercilium and crown-stripe. Conspicuous buff shoulder stripes on darker brown upperparts, many feathers with pale edges and dark brown and chestnut centres; belly whitish with fine barring along flanks. In flight, shows white trailing edge to wings. Often hard to see; secretive, silent and regularly crouches low when approached or resting. Bursts into erratic flight when disturbed, calling harshly and zigzagging high and far (unlike Jack Snipe). Occurs in wetlands. Common passage migrant and winter visitor throughout.

GREAT SNIPE *Gallinago media* 27–29cm

Very similar to Common Snipe and often overlooked, so careful observation needed. All ages similar. Slightly larger and bulkier than Common, with a comparatively shorter bill. Belly and underparts whitish, patterned with fine dark barring throughout. Distinct bold white feathers on outer tail, most notable when taking off or landing. White tips to greater and primary coverts distinctive, both at rest and in flight, when they form prominent wing-bars. Flight less erratic and towering than in Common. Prefers wetland habitats, wet meadows, marshes and ditches. Widespread but very scarce passage migrant, most often seen in spring.

EURASIAN WOODCOCK *Scolopax rusticola* 33–35cm

Pigeon-sized gamebird, not unlike an oversized Common Snipe, with a very short neck and legs, and a rotund, heavy-chested body. Cryptic gold, brown and buff plumage, densely patterned throughout. Bill long, straight, downwards-pointing and pink-grey. Upperparts brown, feathers finely barred dark brown and chestnut, and with pale buff tips. Mantle with some brown-centred feathers. Underparts warm buff with fine rusty-brown barring. Distinctive head shape, with high forehead peaking to a dark double bar across crown, dark eye-stripe and back-set eyes. Often flushed only at close range, taking flight to reveal chestnut rump and tail, and broad, round-tipped wings. Very shy, preferring cover of woodland or scrub in hilly terrain. Rare local resident; common, widespread winter visitor throughout.

▲ Adult summer   ▲ Adult winter in flight

BLACK-TAILED GODWIT *Limosa limosa* 40–44cm

Slender, tall, long-necked, long-legged wader with a very long, almost straight bill on a small head, giving a rather elegant appearance. Summer adult has black-tipped orange bill, cinnamon-red head, neck and upper breast, pale supercilium, and dark lores and crown. Upperparts a mottled mix of grey and black-centred pale cinnamon feathers. Belly white with dark barring, extending along flanks. In flight, white rump, black tail and white wing-bars obvious. Adult winter very plain grey above, plain whitish to grey below. Inhabits both freshwater and saline coastal habitats, often in flocks. Widespread and locally common passage migrant, particularly in spring in larger wetlands in the north-east and west; scarce winter visitor, favouring the west and south.

68

BAR-TAILED GODWIT *Limosa lapponica* 37–39cm

Similar to Black-tailed Godwit, but with shorter legs and a slightly upturned bill. Summer male has more extensive brick-red plumage than Black-tailed, extending to all underparts. Wing and back feathers mottled, buff-edged, pale grey-brown. Eye-stripe and crown dark, supercilium pale. Summer female similar but lighter cinnamon buff on head, neck, breast and along flanks, and white below. Winter adult has dark-centred grey-brown wing and back feathers, giving a streaky appearance, and a dark-tipped pinkish bill and whitish underparts. Juvenile resembles winter adult but more buff-apricot. In flight, wings plain, white rump-patch extends onto lower back and tail is finely barred (see Black-tailed). Scarce passage migrant in spring; scarce winter visitor, mainly to larger estuaries and mudflats along coastal north-east mainland.

WHIMBREL *Numenius phaeopus* 40–42cm

Medium-sized wader, smaller and darker than Eurasian Curlew. Rather uniform, densely mottled brown and cream-buff plumage throughout, darker on back, chest and flanks, with dark brown feathers edged cream. Belly white, breast and neck with many fine, dark brown streaks. Long, slim, dark bill, clearly decurved near tip. Characteristic dark brown crown and eye-stripe, and paler supercilium and central crown-stripe (Eurasian Curlew plain-faced). Legs longish, dark grey. In flight, shows pointed white rump-patch. Call a rapid *tu-tu-tu-tu-tu-tu* trill. Occurs in coastal wetlands. Widespread but scarce migrant throughout in spring and autumn, usually alone or in small groups

EURASIAN CURLEW *Numenius arquata* 50–60cm

Largest European wader, similar to Whimbrel but stockier and longer-legged, with almost comically long, strongly decurved bill. Plumage uniform, strongly mottled brown, grey and buff-cream throughout, with plainer whitish underbelly and undertail. Breast, neck and head with fine, dense dark streaking, head lacking obvious pattering of Whimbrel. In flight, shows a prominent pointed white rump-patch. Legs grey. Call a distinctive *cur-loo*. Favours coastal sites, lagoons, mudflats and saltmarshes, plus inland wetlands. Common and widespread winter visitor and passage migrant throughout.

▲ *Adult summer* ▲ *Adult winter*

SPOTTED REDSHANK *Tringa erythropus* 29–31cm

Elegant long-legged wader with a slim build and fine, medium-length bill that decurves subtly near tip. Summer adult has striking black plumage, many feathers fringed white, and a dark red bill and legs. Winter adult and juvenile more like Common Redshank, but greyer throughout, with strong white lores, pale edges to grey-brown upperparts and cleaner white underparts. In flight, shows elongated white rump but no white trailing edge to wings (unlike Common). Distinct *chui-it* call. Found in coastal wetlands. Fairly common and widespread passage migrant; winter visitor, increasing and particularly common in the north and west.

COMMON REDSHANK *Tringa totanus* 27–29cm

Medium-sized long-legged wader, with bright orange legs and a straight, medium-length, black-tipped orange bill. Only similar species is Spotted Redshank. In flight, shows unique white trailing edge to inner wing and elongated white rump. Summer adult lightly mottled, fairly uniform grey-brown throughout. Upperparts darker, with fine barring to feathers and dense brown speckles and streaks on head, these extending through flanks into whitish underparts. Fine white eye-ring. Winter adult greyer throughout with dark lores and paler supercilium. Juvenile has heavily streaked brown-buff plumage, paler orange legs and a darker bill. A rather alert, nervous wader, easily flushed. Calls readily, a loud, alarmed *teeu-who-who*. Occurs in coastal wetlands. Widespread and locally very common resident throughout.

▼ *Adult summer* ▼ *Adult winter*

MARSH SANDPIPER *Tringa stagnatilis* 22–24cm

Dainty wader with a subtly upturned, needle-like bill and very long legs. Summer adult has stone-grey upperparts with black spots and bars, whitish underparts, and fine dark streaking through head, neck and breast, becoming looser along flanks. Legs dull yellow-green. White rump reaches high along back, obvious in flight. Winter adult plainer grey above, with white underparts, neck and throat, and whitish head with grey cap (see Common Greenshank). Juvenile has brown upperparts, streaked on mantle; pale-fringed dark wing feathers; and clean white underparts. Frequents coastal marshes, lagoons and mudflats, often in small flocks. Fairly common and widespread passage migrant.

COMMON GREENSHANK *Tringa nebularia* 30–33cm

Large, stocky wader with a stout, slightly upcurved bill and an overall heavier appearance than Common Redshank. Long legs and bill base both green-grey. Summer adult brownish grey above with some dark feather centres, white below, and with fine dark streaking and spotting to head, neck and upper breast. Winter adult and juvenile greyer and plainer above, with pale fringes to wing feathers; underparts white. Streaking to head, neck and upper breast finer and reduced. In flight, uniform brownish wings and extended white rump obvious. Call a strong triple *tchew-tchew-tchew*. Frequents brackish, saline and freshwater habitats, on coasts and inland. Fairly common and widespread passage migrant; scarce winter visitor. Most numerous in larger wetlands of Thrace, Macedonia and western Greece.

▼ *Adult winter*

GREEN SANDPIPER *Tringa ochropus* 21–24cm

Similar to Common Sandpiper, but larger and with more contrasting dark upperparts and white underparts. In flight, white rump and dark wings distinct. Upperparts dark grey-brown, fairly uniform with some pale speckling. Head, neck and upper breast dark grey-brown with fine darker streaks, ending in breast-band before clean white underparts. Legs and longish bill grey-green. Supercilium (not extending past eye) and eye-ring white, contrasting with dark lores. Flight call a repeated *twit-a-wit*. Prefers freshwater and brackish wetlands, ditches and pools with close marginal cover. Fairly common and widespread passage migrant and winter visitor, present almost year-round.

WOOD SANDPIPER *Tringa glareola* 19–21cm

Differs from similar Common Redshank in smaller size and yellow-green legs, and from Green Sandpiper in longer, more obviously yellow legs and browner-grey upperparts speckled with numerous pale brown-buff spots. White tail has narrow dark bars. Prominent pale supercilium extends clearly behind eye. Neck and breast pale with diffused grey-brown streaking; lacks breast-band. In flight, upperwing uniform and dark, and rump white (unlike Common Sandpiper), and underwing much paler than in Green Sandpiper. Prefers well-vegetated freshwater and brackish wetlands and marshland. Very common and widespread passage migrant, most numerous in spring.

COMMON SANDPIPER *Actitis hypoleucos* 19–21cm

Medium-sized wader, readily identified by shape and behaviour. Relatively short neck and legs, slender body and longish tail. Holds itself semi-crouched. Upperparts pale grey-brown. Distinct grey breast-band separated from grey wings by white around carpal joint, this extending into underparts. Legs and relatively short, straight bill both dull greenish grey. Supercilium white and lores dark. In flight, shows white wing-bar and no white rump (unlike Green Sandpiper). Flight call a repeated, high-pitched *swee-swee-swee*. Distinctive flickering flight on rapid, stiff-winged, shallow wingbeats and short glides. Habit of bobbing body and pumping rear is characteristic. Favours rivers and lakes, and coastal wetlands on passage. Fairly common and widespread passage migrant throughout; rare local summer visitor.

RUDDY TURNSTONE *Arenaria interpres* 22–24cm

Dumpy, medium-sized wader with short orange legs, a broad-based dark bill and a rather pied appearance. Summer male shows extensive chestnut-orange and black mantle, back and flight feathers. Underparts white, and head white with black face, neck and breast-band. Crown white with very fine black streaks. Summer female similar but duller, with less orange to upperparts and less defined facial banding. Winter adult with more uniform brown to head, broad blackish-brown breast-band, varied mottled brown upperparts and clean white underparts. In flight, appears very black and white with obvious black band across white tail, and white wing-bars and back patch. Favours rocky coastal habitats, shingle beaches and tidelines; may gather on wet grassland on passage. Fairly common, widespread passage migrant.

▼ *Adult breeding*   ▼ *Adult non-breeding*

ARCTIC SKUA *Stercorarius parasiticus* 41–46cm

Also known as Parasitic Jaeger. Graceful yet robust seabird, rather like a gull or large tern, with pointed wings, white primary patches and strikingly long central tail feathers. Two colour morphs. Dark phase chocolate brown, often with lighter buff face. Pale phase has dark cap, upperparts, wings and tail, contrasting with pale buff-cream face, collar and underparts, and broken dusky breast-band and undertail. Juvenile mottled brown and buff throughout, with shorter central tail feathers. Kleptoparasite, stealing food from other birds. Occurs along coasts. Widespread but scarce passage migrant, mainly along the coasts of Thrace and Macedonia.

BLACK-HEADED GULL *Larus ridibundus* 34–37cm

Small, slender, bold gull. Summer adult has chocolate-brown hood, white crescent behind eye, dark red bill and bright red legs. Uniform pale grey above and white below, with black primary tips to long, pointed wings. In winter adult, bill brighter orange-red and tipped black, hood replaced by two dark spots on side of white head. Juvenile has mixed gingery-brown markings to back and wings, and black band across white tail. All ages show white wedge to leading edge of wing and black primary tips. First-summer (with brown hood) and first-winter have additional black tips to secondaries and dark barring across upperwing. Found around coastal and inland wetlands. Rare, local resident, with a colony at Lake Kerkini. Very common, widespread winter visitor.

▼ *Summer adult*
▶ *Winter adult (top), juvenile (below)*

▲ Summer adult ▲ In flight

SLENDER-BILLED GULL *Larus genei* 42–44cm

Elegant, regal-looking gull. Summer adult has pure white head, white breast (often flushed pink), dark red bill (appearing black). Legs dark red; eye pale, rimmed bright red. Winter adult similar to winter Black-headed Gull, but larger, with longer body, bill and neck; faint (if any) face spot and yellow-white iris. Juvenile and first-winter have pale orange legs and bill. Best identification feature at all ages is long bill and long, sloping forehead, giving distinctive smooth, slender outline. Prefers brackish water, coastal lagoons, harbours and shallow wetlands; often in flocks. Rare local resident; locally common winter visitor and passage migrant.

MEDITERRANEAN GULL *Larus melanocephalus* 36–38cm

Larger and stockier than Black-headed Gull, with deep, chunky bill. Summer adult has red bill with black-and-yellow tip, contrasting with brown-black hood and white eye crescent. Plumage pale grey above and white below, wings all white in flight, legs bright red. In winter adult, hood replaced by broken black mask, eyes smoky and legs duller. Immature has variable black markings on primaries, evident in flight and at rest; legs and bill dark. Juvenile has extensive black-brown to upperparts, not unlike Common Gull. Widespread, locally common coastal resident. Congregates in coastal breeding colonies in spring, favouring large wetlands in the north.

▼ Adult winter ▼ Adult summer

AUDOUIN'S GULL *Larus audouinii* 48–52cm

Dainty, medium-sized gull. Adult like a large Yellow-legged Gull, but close views reveal smaller, dark red bill, green-grey legs and dark eyes. Upperparts pale grey, head and underparts white. In flight, white spots along black primary-tip wedge appear as 'string of pearls', and upperwing has very narrow white trailing edge. Juvenile pale-faced, with smoky-brown scaling throughout upperparts, black tail-band and U-shaped white rump-patch. First-winter has whiter head and paler grey on back; bill and legs dull grey. Nests colonially on rocky outcrops; found around mainland coasts during non-breeding months. Scarce local resident, breeding restricted to southern Aegean islands.

COMMON GULL *Larus canus* 40–42cm

Also known as Mew Gull. Smaller than European Herring Gull, with softer features and round head. Summer adult grey above (darker than European Herring), with obvious white spots to primary tips. Head and underparts white. Legs yellowy green; bill yellow, lacking red spot of European Herring; eyes dark, rimmed red. Winter adult has grey mottling on white head and grey band through dull green bill. Juvenile scaly above with pale-fringed brown upperparts, whitish underparts with speckled dark markings on breast and flanks, and dark bill. In flight, black tail-band, white rump and more extensive black to upperwing obvious. First-winter has grey mantle, paler bill with cleaner white underparts. Found on inland freshwater lakes and along coasts. Fairly common, local winter visitor.

▼ *Summer adult*
▶ *Winter adult (top), juvenile (below)*

LESSER BLACK-BACKED GULL *Larus fuscus* 52–64cm

Large, slim, long-winged gull. Summer adult distinctive, with slate-grey upperparts, pure white underparts, contrasting black primary tips, and bright yellow legs. Large bill large yellow with red tip to lower mandible. Eyes pale, rimmed red. Winter adult has dusky streaks around head and nape, and duller legs. Juvenile brown-grey throughout, with scaly pale fringes to upperparts and brown-grey mottling to underparts. Bill dark, legs pink. Second-winter develops grey to mantle and paler underparts. Third-winter with grey to mantle and wings, and dirtier mottling to head and breast. Widespread, locally fairly common passage migrant and winter visitor throughout inland fresh waters and coasts.

EUROPEAN HERRING GULL *Larus argentatus* 55–64cm

Large, sturdy gull. Summer adult upperparts paler grey than in other gulls. Wing-tips black with white spots to primaries, underparts white. Legs pale pink, large bill yellow with red tip to lower mandible. Winter adult has heavily streaked head and nape. Juvenile and first-year difficult to separate from Lesser Black-backed Gull and Yellow-legged Gull, but face generally darker. Also similar to juvenile and first-winter Common Gull, but structurally different and Common has black tail-band and white rump. Second-winter develops distinctive pale grey mantle, making identification easier. Widespread but fairly rare winter visitor to inland fresh waters and coasts.

▲ *Adult summer*
▼ *2nd winter*

▲ *Adult*   ▲ *Second year*

YELLOW-LEGGED GULL *Larus michahellis* 55–64cm

Mediterranean counterpart to European Herring Gull, similar in both adult and subadult plumages. Summer adult differs in having yellow legs, smaller white spots on black outer primaries, larger red spot on lower mandible and darker grey upperparts. Winter adult has restricted streaking around white head. Juvenile and first-year hard to distinguish from European Herring and Lesser Black-backed gulls of same ages, but wings darker, bill all black, head paler with dark eye markings, tail-band neat and black, and rump pale. Similar to adult Lesser Black-backed but back paler. Often around coastal human habitation. Nests along coasts and, less often, inland. Very common and widespread resident.

CASPIAN GULL *Larus cachinnans* 57–67cm

Large, elegant gull, similar to European Herring and Lesser Black-backed gulls, but with comparatively longer legs and neck. Distinguished by flat forehead, angled crown and longer, evenly shaped bill. Eye appears small and dark. Adult has more white spots than other species and white extends into restricted black primary tips. Legs and bill variable dull green-yellow in winter, brighter in summer. Tip of lower mandible shows red spot in summer, and red spot with black comma mark in winter. Juvenile uniform, with pale fringes to all darker feathers; lacks pale notches and indentations shown in juvenile European Herring. First-winter often has whiter head and underparts than European Herring. Fairly common winter visitor and passage migrant along coasts.

▲ *Adult winter* ▶ *Adult spring in flight (top),
Juvenile in flight (below)*

LITTLE GULL *Hydrocoloeus minutus* 25–27cm

Dainty with a buoyant flight. Summer adult has a black hood but lacks white eye crescent and brown tones of similar Black-headed Gull. Underparts white, often with pink flush; upperparts pale grey. Distinctive dusky underwing and white trailing edge to wing visible from above and below. Small bill and legs red. In adult winter, dark hood replaced with blackish cap and black ear-spot. Juvenile has extensive black-centred feathers on upperparts, appearing barred, and black around nape, black tail-band and obvious black 'W' to upperwing in flight. First-winter has less black on upperparts but retains black 'W'. Frequents coastal wetlands, harbours and inshore lakes, usually in small groups. Widespread but uncommon passage migrant; scarce winter visitor.

LITTLE TERN *Sternula albifrons* 22–24cm

Tiny, front-heavy yet agile tern with a long bill, forked tail and narrow wings. Summer adult has silvery-grey upperparts with black outer primaries. Face white with contrasting black lores and crown. Bill yellow with black tip, legs orangey yellow. Winter adult has black bill, lacks black to lores and has more extensive white to forehead. Juvenile similar, but with brown-black bars and scaling to upperparts, duskier face and duller legs. Found on coasts; often hovers and dives for fish. Widespread and locally common summer visitor and passage migrant.

GULL-BILLED TERN *Gelochelidon nilotica* 35–38cm

Large tern, similar in size to Sandwich Tern but with a narrower body and shorter tail, broader wings and thicker all-black bill. Summer adult has pale grey upperparts, pure white underparts, full black crown extending along back of nape, and black legs. Winter adult and juvenile have broad black band through eye on otherwise white head. Hunts for insects on the wing and from inshore and coastal waterbodies. Scarce local summer visitor, with a couple of small breeding colonies in the west and north-east; more common and widespread passage migrant.

WHISKERED TERN *Chlidonias hybrida* 23–25cm

Larger and more robust than other marsh terns, with longer legs and a weightier bill. Summer adult dark grey throughout, with white face, black crown extending into nape, and dark red bill and legs. Tail short with shallow fork, rump grey. Adult winter paler grey, with a finely streaked crown, white forehead and dark ear-coverts. Juvenile has whitish underparts and grey upperparts with boldly scaled brown-and-black patterning on mantle and back. Frequents both freshwater and saline coastal and inland habitats. Common passage migrant, often in mixed flocks; rare and very local summer visitor.

▲ *Adult summer*

▲ *Adult summer*

BLACK TERN *Chlidonias niger* 22–24cm

Small, dainty marsh tern with characteristic buoyant, 'dipping' flight. Body slim, bill and legs dark. Summer adult striking, with smoky-grey mantle and wings, and jet-black upperparts from head to underbelly contrasting with white vent and undertail. Underwing pale grey; tail short, forked. In winter adult, black upperparts replaced with white, leaving black only on hindcrown and ear-coverts; distinctive curved, dark grey shoulder-patch. Juvenile similar, but mantle and wings scaly, with dark grey feathering fringed pale brown-cream. Seen in freshwater habitats and on coasts. Very rare local summer visitor; common passage migrant.

WHITE-WINGED TERN *Chlidonias leucopterus* 20–23cm

Very delicate marsh tern, similar to Black Tern but with smaller bill and broader wings. Summer adult shows conspicuous white rump and forewing in flight, and contrasting jet-black upperparts and almost black back at rest. Underwing-coverts jet black. Winter adult has pale grey upperparts, white underparts, and dark ear-coverts and hindcrown streaking on otherwise white head. Juvenile resembles juvenile Black Tern but lacks grey shoulder-patch, has darker grey back and white rump evident in flight. Occurs in brackish and freshwater habitats. Common, widespread passage migrant, much more numerous in spring.

▼ *Adult summer*   ▼ *Adult summer*

SANDWICH TERN *Sterna sandvicensis* 36–41cm

Large tern with a front-heavy appearance, long wings, and a short tail and legs. Forehead low and elongated, crest blunt and dishevelled, bill long and slender. Summer adult has yellow tip to black bill, black crown and crest, and black legs. Upperparts pale grey with some black to primary tips only. Underparts white. Winter adult and first-winter have white forehead and restricted black crown, giving masked appearance. Juvenile has full dusky-brown cap, all-black bill, dark barring to back and dark edges to most upperpart feathers. Occurs along coasts. Very rare local resident; widespread winter visitor and passage migrant.

COMMON TERN *Sterna hirundo* 31–35cm

Medium-sized tern with a long, forked tail. Summer adult has a black-tipped red-orange bill (all blood-red in similar Arctic Tern; not illustrated), short red legs, pale grey upperparts, white underparts, light grey tones to belly and smart black cap extending onto nape. Wings long and slender, with darker grey primaries towards tips. In winter adult, black cap partly replaced with white forehead and bill darkens. Juvenile has white forehead, black mask and carpal joint bar, scaly dark edges to grey or ginger-brown upperparts, and pink-orange legs and bill base. Breeds colonially in coastal and inland wetlands, where it is also found during migration. Widespread, locally common summer visitor and passage migrant.

EUROPEAN TURTLE DOVE *Streptopelia turtur* 26–28cm

Rather shy, dainty dove with unmistakable plumage. Adult has scaly orange-brown edges to dark-centred feathers on upperparts. Proportionately small head 'dove' grey, becoming dirty pink through neck and breast, light apricot on lower breast, white on belly. Red eye-ring and small square black-and-white striped patch on neck collar visible at close range. Bill grey, legs pink. Tail striking when fanned, with white-tipped black outer-tail feathers above and below. Juvenile similar but duller, with extensive softer-toned scaling to upperparts; lacks red eye-ring and black-and-white collar-patch. Song a mournfully soft 'purring'. Favours open deciduous woodland and farmland. Common, widespread but declining summer resident and passage migrant.

EURASIAN COLLARED DOVE *Streptopelia decaocto* 31–33cm

Medium-sized dove with a slender body, long tail and small rounded head. Adult has pale beige-brown upperparts with black primaries, and pale pink-buff underparts, broken by black bar across back of neck collar. Bill grey, legs pink, eye red. Juvenile similar but duller and lacks black bar on collar. All ages have buff-grey tail with white tips to outer-tail feathers (see European Turtle Dove). Song a soft, melancholic, repeated *doo-dooo-do*. Favours areas around human habitation. Common and widespread resident.

COMMON WOOD PIGEON *Columba palumbus* 40–42cm

Large, portly pigeon with broad wings, a long tail and small head. Adult has storm-grey upperparts and head, pinkish-mauve breast and underparts, and paler grey-white towards undertail. Distinctive white patch and smaller glossy green area on collar. Bill small, stout and yellowy, with raised white area on top of upper mandible. Eye small, straw yellow. In flight, shows distinctive white band across wings. Makes loud wing-clapping when flushed. Breeds in woodlands, parks and gardens; also closely associated with oak woodlands and in winter often congregates en masse in open cultivated areas. Common and widespread resident.

COMMON CUCKOO *Cuculus canorus* 32–34cm

Slender bird, not unlike a small falcon. Often perches with long, rounded tail raised, long wings drooped and body tipped forward on short legs. Male slate grey above, with paler grey head, neck and upper breast. Underparts white with dark barring. Eyes yellow, legs and base of short bill grey. Female similar, but chestnut-brown 'hepatic' form can occur. Juvenile brown above, white below, with barring throughout. Lays eggs in other birds' nests; on hatching, Common Cuckoo chick ejects other eggs so is reared alone by host parents. Found in wide variety of open countryside and wooded habitats, depending on particular host species. *Cu-koo* notes repeated by male in spring song. Fairly widespread, scarce summer visitor; widespread, fairly common passage migrant.

BARN OWL *Tyto alba* 33–35cm

Unmistakable slender, long-legged owl. Upperparts and head warm brown and grey with tiny black-and-white flecks. Face a heart-shaped white disc; eyes small, black and beady eyes, bill very small and hooked. Underparts and underwing white. Appears almost ghostly when most commonly sighted in half-light of dusk. Hunts mainly at night. Dark-breasted Barn Owl (*T. a. guttata*) subspecies also occurs; heavier brown-grey above and brown-orange below. Call a haunting, repeated shriek. Frequents open areas, farmland and olive groves; nests in farm outbuildings, sometimes in villages and towns. Fairly scarce but widespread resident throughout lowlands.

EURASIAN SCOPS OWL *Otus scops* 19–20cm

Very small grey-brown owl with prominent ear-tufts and cryptic plumage, blending in against tree bark and branches. Plumage a variable mix of grey, brown and rufous, with fine black streaks throughout, and white spotting to flight feathers and shoulder braces. Eyes yellow. Nocturnal. Familiar repeated, whistling *tyuu* night call in spring and summer. Nocturnal, roosting by day, often with an upright pose and erect ear-tufts. Inhabits open woodlands, gardens, parks, olive groves and even villages and towns. Often nests in old tree-holes. Two races occur: *O. s. scops*, fairly common, widespread resident; *O. s. cycladum*, partial migrant and resident in parts of south and some islands.

EURASIAN EAGLE-OWL *Bubo bubo* 60–75cm

Enormous brown owl, the largest owl in Europe. Upperparts dark brown with mottled black streaks and bars. Ear-tufts conspicuous, long, black and brown; eyes large, bright orange. Underparts paler, warm buff-brown with fine dark bars and bold streaking, the latter denser around collar and breast, lighter towards underbelly. Tail short, square-ended and barred. Nocturnal. Song a low, flat, booming *oohu-oohu-oohu*. Prefers open habitats for hunting; also rocky terrain, gorges, cliffs and old quarries, sometimes near rural habitation. Widespread but scarce resident throughout mainland and on a few Aegean islands.

LITTLE OWL *Athene noctua* 21–23cm

A small owl, slightly larger than Scops, with no ear-tufts and longer legs. Upperparts warm brown, with blotchy white patches on wings, fine white streaks on crown, white eyebrows over yellow eyes, and white around throat and collar. Underparts dusky white with warm brown streaks, denser on breast. Call often a sharp, repeated *keew*. Active by day and night, often perching in the open on rocks. Characteristic tall posture and 'squat-and-bob' action when alarmed or excited. Flight low, direct, showing short wings and tail. Found in both rural and urban open areas, farmland, orchards, rocky terrain, out buildings. Fairly common, widespread resident. Browner race *A. n. indigena* also occurs throughout.

TAWNY OWL *Strix aluco* 37–39cm

Medium-sized nocturnal owl. Adult has a large rounded head and wings, barrel-shaped body and short tail. Upperparts mottled brown, grey, buff and white, with fine black streaks throughout. Underparts paler buff-grey with bolder streaking and deep brown bars across wing feathers, often visible in flight. Face plain, with small yellow bill and large black eyes; central brown crown-stripe bordered by whitish buff. Call a sharp, repeated *ke-wick*; song a typical hoot. Often hunched and inconspicuous against tree trunks by day; hunts by 'perch-and-pounce' attack. Nests in tree-holes. Found in woodland. Fairly common and widespread resident throughout mainland and some northern Aegean islands.

LONG-EARED OWL *Asio otus* 35–37cm

Medium-sized, narrow-bodied nocturnal owl with long wings and pronounced ear-tufts. Upperparts mottled grey, brown and buff, with dark brown streaks and speckling. Underparts buff with dark streaks throughout. Eyes bright orange, facial disc buff. In flight, upperwing shows many dark bars and buff patch at base of primaries, underwing cream with dark comma mark. Juvenile whitish grey, face dark; perches away from nest when very young. Two distinctive postures adopted: tall, camouflaged pose with long features when roosting or threatened; and more rotund, fluffed-up, compact pose when relaxed. Often roosts communally in winter. Favours pine trees, copses and forest edges bordering open habitats. Fairly common, widespread resident and winter visitor.

▼ *Adult*　　　　　　　▼ *Chick*

EUROPEAN NIGHTJAR *Caprimulgus europaeus* 26–28cm

Highly cryptic plumage of intricate grey, black and brown-buff markings. Narrow, slender body, long tail and wings, and large head. Dark bill tiny, legs very short. In flight, male shows obvious white patches near wing-tips (lacking in female and juvenile) and outer tail. Song unusual, a loud, reeling *churr* that can last for hours, interspersed with occasional wing-claps. Roosts horizontally on branches or on ground by day; agile aerial hunter from dusk. Prefers dry, open stony areas with scattered trees, sand dunes and dry fringes of coastal marshes. Common and widespread summer visitor and passage migrant.

ALPINE SWIFT *Tachymarptis melba* 20–22cm

Largest swift, with a powerful flight. Longer-winged and significantly larger than Common and Pallid swifts. Readily identified by large white belly-patch and white throat (visible in close views), separated by brown necklace. Upperparts brown; tail tapered, subtly forked. Call a long, high-pitched, chattering trill. Often forms large, wide-roaming flocks when hunting on the wing. Nests colonially in buildings and rocky cliffs. Common and widespread summer visitor and passage migrant. Breeds throughout.

COMMON SWIFT *Apus apus* 16–17cm

Larger than swallows and martins, with dark plumage, distinctive scythe-shaped wings and tapering, forked tail. Adult chocolate brown with small, poorly defined paler area to throat and forehead. Juvenile similar but paler; can show scaling on body, like Pallid Swift. Often seen hunting for insects low over wetlands, or in fast-flying 'screaming' parties in urban areas. Perches only at nest, otherwise always airborne. Nests under roof tiles and eaves, rarely in natural sites. Very common, widespread summer visitor and passage migrant.

PALLID SWIFT *Apus pallidus* 16–17cm

Very similar to Common Swift, but with more laboured flight and marginally broader body and wings, particularly at primary tips. Whitish patch on throat and forehead larger, and dark 'mask' surrounding eye contrasts with paler brown head. Paler brown inner secondaries on upperwing contrast with dark brown 'saddle' on back. Key feature in all ages is pale-fringed scaling throughout body and upperwing-coverts. Often found at same sites as Common, but less abundant. Frequents more coastal and low-lying areas, and can often breed later and stay later. Common and widespread summer visitor.

▲ Adult female

▲ Adult male

COMMON KINGFISHER *Alcedo atthis* 16–17cm

Coloration and size enable easy identification. Small and compact, with short body, wings and tail, large head and weighty, dagger-shaped bill. Brilliant blue-aquamarine upperparts with lighter electric blue to rump and back. Mottled blue crown, blue facial stripe, orange-and-white ear-coverts and white throat. Underparts bright orange, short legs red. Bill dark but lower mandible orange in female. Flies fast and low, often just a flash of colour. Prefers brackish and freshwater habitats. Nest in holes on riverbanks. Common, widespread winter visitor; scarce local resident in central and northern mainland and occasionally larger islands.

EUROPEAN BEE-EATER *Merops apiaster* 27–29cm

Slender, exotic-looking, multicoloured bird. Adult an unmistakable mix of rich chestnut orange and yellow on upperparts, and clean yellow throat separated by black band from dazzling aquamarine underparts and tail. Bill slender, dark and curved, face with jet-black eye-stripe and ear-coverts, tail long with longer central feathers. Juvenile similar but duller. Call a soft *prrut*. Favours open habitats with scattered scrub; nests colonially in holes in sandy riverbanks and cliffs. Widespread, locally common summer visitor and passage migrant, with populations decreasing further south. Migrates in flocks.

▼ Adult

▼ In flight

▲ Adult

▲ Adult in flight

EUROPEAN ROLLER *Coracias garrulus* 30–32cm

Large, stocky bird with a top-heavy head, strong bill and striking plumage. Back and part of wings chestnut brown, contrasting with turquoise-blue head, forewing and underparts. In flight from above, shows chestnut back, turquoise coverts and black flight feathers. Inner tail royal blue, outer tail turquoise. Underwing royal blue with pale blue coverts. Juvenile similar but duller, with brown streaks through turquoise upperparts. Flies straight, with short, purposeful beats. Prefers open, dry countryside. Scarce local summer visitor and uncommon passage migrant; breeding confined to the north Greece and some southerly Aegean islands.

HOOPOE *Upupa epops* 26–28cm

Unmistakable medium-sized bird, with a large crest on a small head, slender body, rounded wings and long, thin, decurved bill. Head and body coral pink. Wings, rump and tail black with white bars throughout; black and white particularly striking in flight, when wide 'butterfly' wings extend fully. Crest long, often held flat but can be raised into coral-coloured fan with black tips. Song a rather hollow *hoop-hoop-hoop*. Frequents open countryside, short grassland, farmland and olive groves. Usually nests in tree-holes, or sometimes rock crevices or old buildings. Fairly common and widespread summer visitor and passage migrant.

EURASIAN WRYNECK *Jynx torquilla* 16–17cm

Secretive, cryptically plumaged small woodpecker. Bill small and pointed, body slender and tail fairly long. Plumage an intricate array of grey, brown, black, white and buff, resembling tree bark. Head grey, with long, decurved brown eye-stripe; nape, back and tail grey, with dark bars to tail and single dark band along back. Wings brown with fine black-and-white speckling. Throat buff and underparts white, both with fine dark barring. Does not use tail when climbing like other woodpeckers, instead perching horizontally on branches and ground. Frequents open woodland, roadside verges, gardens and orchards. Scarce and local resident; fairly common and widespread passage migrant.

EUROPEAN GREEN WOODPECKER *Picus viridis* 31–33cm

Large, robust woodpecker with a strong bill. Upperparts and tail mossy green, with white spotting to blackish outer primaries and a striking yellow-green rump, obvious in flight. Red crown, black mask around pale eye, and black moustachial stripe with red centre on male, all black in female. Rest of head and underparts pale cream with a green hue, and dark barring on flanks. Juvenile similar, but with dark spotting to pale head and underparts, and lacks black face mask. Often found on ground, but has a strong, bold flight. Found in mixed open woodland, orchards, pastures and grassland. Call a projecting *yaffle*. Widespread and locally fairly common resident in northern and central mainland.

BLACK WOODPECKER
Dryocopus martius 43cm

Very large, distinctive woodpecker, with a powerful black-tipped ivory bill, all-black plumage and contrasting white eye. Crown red in male; red restricted to hindcrown in female. Proportionately thin neck on oversized head and robust body. Flight flapping, heavy-winged, straight. Flight call a loud *krrr-krrr-krrr*. Found in mixed wood-land habitats in mountains as far south as Mt Parnassus, where it prefers mature Greek Fir (*Abies cephalonica*) woodlands. Fairly widespread but scarce resident, confined to mainland.

SYRIAN WOODPECKER *Dendrocopos syriacus* 22–23cm

Distinctly black-and-white woodpecker, very similar to the rare, local Great Spotted Woodpecker (*D. major*; not illustrated). Hindcrown with small red patch in male, all black in female. Upperparts mainly black, with large white shoulder-patches and white spotting on black flight feathers. Underparts and head off-white, with black cap, nape and moustachial stripe, the latter extending around shoulder but not to black nape-patch (unlike in adult Great Spotted Woodepcker). Vent pale pinkish red, flanks very lightly streaked. Favours mixed open woodland, poplar plantations, farmland with scattered trees, orchards and gardens. Fairly common and widespread resident with a northerly bias.

MIDDLE SPOTTED WOODPECKER
Dendrocopos medius 20–22cm

Medium-sized pied woodpecker, similar to Syrian Woodpecker. Upperparts black with white shoulder-patch and white spotting on black flight feathers (appears as white bars on closed wings). Crown red; face, forehead and cheeks plain white (lacks black moustachial stripe), and has small black eye. Underparts whitish with dark flank streaking, yellowish wash to belly, and pinkish-red underbelly and vent. Prefers oak woodland and, on Lesvos, Sweet Chestnut (*Castanea sativa*) woodland and olive groves. Nests in tree-holes. Fairly common and widespread resident across mainland Greece, Lesvos and Chios.

WHITE-BACKED WOODPECKER *Dendrocopos leucotos* 24–26cm

Largest of the European pied woodpeckers, with a relatively long neck and bill. In flight, shows barred white patch on lower back. Long horizontal white bar replaces oval white shoulder-patches of Middle Spotted, Syrian and Great Spotted (*D. major*; not illustrated) woodpeckers. Crown red in male, all black in female. Moustachial stripe reaches bill. Underparts with dark streaking throughout, not restricted to flanks. Favours montane areas with mixed forests bordering lakes and rivers. Widespread but rare resident.

LESSER SPOTTED WOODPECKER *Dendrocopos minor* 14–15cm

Easily identifiable, being a third smaller than other pied woodpeckers. Black upperparts strongly barred white, right across wings and back. Underparts off-white, with many dark streaks along breast-sides and flanks. Vent off-white. Crown red in male, white in female. Repetitive, loud *keek* call and distinctive drumming in spring. Rather fluttery flight, often for short distances at height between treetops; rarely seen at ground level. Found in woodlands and orchards. Fairly widespread but scarce resident; absent from south mainland and the islands.

CALANDRA LARK *Melanocorypha calandra* 18–19cm

Robust, thickset lark with broad wings, a short tail and notably heavy yellow-brown bill. Upperparts tawny brown with dark streaking, underparts cream-white with buff flanks. Mottled tawny-brown crown and cheeks contrast with whitish supercilium, eye-ring and throat. Very distinctive but variable black patch on side of breast. Legs pinkish. In flight, dark underwing contrasts with white trailing edge and white tail sides. Call a buzzing trill; characteristic fast, chirping song, often performed while hanging in the air at height. Prefers dry, open stony habitats, grassland, farmland and sand dunes. Widespread and locally common resident with a patchy distribution; irregular and scarce passage migrant in spring.

GREATER SHORT-TOED LARK *Calandrella brachydactyla* 13–14cm

Pale, unobtrusive lark with a broad-based finch-like bill. Upperparts sandy brown with dark streaking and pale feather fringes. Long tertial feathers nearly reach primary tips. Very dark centres to medium coverts appear as a narrow bar. Sandy-brown crown (which can appear raised), and light brown cheeks on otherwise very pale face. Underparts white with a little buff to breast and occasional hint of black patch to breast side. Legs pinkish. Call a short *trilp*. Prefers flat, dry, open terrain with sparse vegetation, dry saltmarshes and grazed pastures. Common and widespread summer visitor and passage migrant.

CRESTED LARK *Galerida cristata* 17cm

Appears bulkier and shorter-tailed than Eurasian Skylark, with a strong, subtly decurved bill and a spiky crest that protrudes from head when flattened. Upperparts sandy grey-brown with pale fringes to dark-centred feathers. Head sandy brown with dark moustache and dark edging to buff eye-ring. Crest finely streaked, throat and partial collar white. Underparts white with dark streaking to breast and buff flanks. Wing lacks white trailing edge of Eurasian Skylark, and underwing and outer tail show rusty brown in flight. Legs pink. Call a soft, fluty *twee-tee-too*. Prefers stony lowland habitats, roadsides and waste ground, seen perching on barbed wire and posts. Familiar common and widespread resident.

WOODLARK *Lullula arborea* 15cm

Delicate lark with a slender bill and short tail. Upperparts mid-brown and buff, feathers with dark central streaks. Head short, with an often inconspicuous crest, dark-streaked brown crown. Long, pale buff supercilium, dark-bordered rufous ear-coverts, black moustache, and white on throat and neck. Dark streaks across breast, white underparts. Distinct black-and-white pattern on wing edge, most obvious in flight. Tail brown, tipped white. Song a fluty *tew-leet*. Prefers dry, open habitats with scattered trees. Fairly common and widespread resident, numbers swelling in winter with arrivals from north.

EURASIAN SKYLARK *Alauda arvensis* 18–19cm

Large, slim lark with longish legs, wings and tail, and short crest. Upperparts brown, with pale brown fringes to dark-centred feathers. Head pale with dark streaks to crown and buff ear-coverts. Face with indistinct markings and pale supercilium/eye-ring. Breast buff, streaked dark, contrasting with white belly. In flight, white trailing edge to wings and tail sides is diagnostic. Often hovers before landing. Call a *chirrup*; song loud, varied and melodious, performed at height in hovering flight. Prefers open inland and coastal cultivated areas. Fairly common but local resident; common and widespread winter visitor. Breeding is localised, with a north mainland bias.

HORNED LARK *Eremophila alpestris* 14–17cm

Distinctive lark, similar in size to Eurasian Skylark. Male has black mask-like pattern on lemon-yellow face, black 'horns' on black cap, and black markings from bill base to eye, down cheek and into black breast-band. Upperparts pale sandy brown with dark-centred feathers. Underparts white, flanks sandy buff. Bill grey with a black tip, legs dark. Outer-tail feathers black. Female duller, with restricted black, no horns and paler yellow to face. Juvenile with spangled black, white and brown upperparts, diffuse black-and-yellow head markings, no horns, and a pinkish bill and legs. Favours limestone slopes and rocky terrain above the treeline. Fairly widespread but scarce resident, breeding in mainland mountains.

SAND MARTIN *Riparia riparia* 12cm

Small brown-and-white hirundine with a lightly forked tail, rather slight build and long, pointed wings. Upperparts light brown, face with white throat and partial white collar, small bill and very short legs dark. Underparts whitish apart from light brown breast-band, which is diagnostic visible at distance. Juvenile similar, but underparts more buff and upperparts scaly with pale edges to feathers. Call a rather indistinct, grating *tschrd*. Very rapid, agile flight. Commonly seen hunting over freshwater and brackish wetlands. Nests colonially in excavated holes in sandy riverbanks and quarries. On passage, often roosts in large flocks in reedbeds with Barn Swallows. Widespread and locally common summer visitor; very common passage migrant.

▼ *Adult*   ▼ *Adult in flight*

EURASIAN CRAG MARTIN *Ptyonoprogne rupestris* 14–15cm

Robust brown hirundine with broad, pointed wings and a subtly forked tail. Upperparts and head dusky brown, underparts dusky cream apart from faint dark streaking to throat and darker brown vent. In flight, shows characteristic white 'mirrors' on fanned tail. Underwing pale brown with contrasting chocolate-brown coverts. Favours mainland Greece and the Aegean Islands at some altitude. Breeds inland and in coastal rocky areas, cliffs, gorges and outcrops. Nests singularly or in loose colonies. Fairly common and widespread partial migrant.

BARN SWALLOW *Hirundo rustica* 17–19cm

Familiar species with a narrow body, pointed wings and a highly forked tail with tail-streamers (longer in male). In adult, upperparts almost black with a striking blue sheen in good light, forehead and throat deep red bordering black upper breast-band. Underparts white, from breast to undertail. Small white 'mirrors' visible on tail when fanned. Juvenile duskier, lacks blue sheen, forehead and throat more orange, and tail-streamers short. Breeds in both natural and human-created habitats; nest is an open mud bowl. Outside the breeding season, roosts colonially and hunts in parties, often low over wetlands. Very common and widespread summer visitor and passage migrant.

RED-RUMPED SWALLOW *Cecropis daurica* 16–17cm
....
Similar to Barn Swallow but obvious rusty-red rump is diagnostic (can look
white at distance). In adult, upperparts and head cap brownish black with
a blue sheen. Nape and sides of face pale reddish brown, throat and
underparts dusky cream with dark streaks. Undertail-coverts black (white in
Barn Swallow), underwing pale grey with dusky-pink coverts. Juvenile
similar, but duller and with scaly upperparts. Prefers high mountains,
hillsides, cliffs, and slopes with open woodland and adjacent pastures.
Often nests on bridges and old rural buildings; nest is a closed mud
structure with a tunnel entrance. Widespread and locally common summer
visitor, although always in smaller numbers than Barn Swallow.

COMMON HOUSE MARTIN *Delichon urbicum* 12–13cm
....
Unmistakable, almost black-and-white hirundine, with a shallow forked
tail and white rump. Adult upperparts and hood almost black with a faint
blue gloss, except on duller wings. Rump-patch square and white.
Underparts pure white and underwing pale grey, contrasting with black
undertail. At close range when on ground, white feathered legs visible.
Juvenile similar but duller. Often seen hunting insects over water. Nests
colonially in a variety of natural and human-created habitats; nest is a
mud cup. Common and widespread summer visitor.

▼ *Adult*   ▼ *Juvenile in flight*

TAWNY PIPIT *Anthus campestris* 16–17cm

Large, slender pipit with an upright stance. Adult has a pale sandy-brown back, mantle and nape. Wings, including coverts, dark-centred, with tawny-brown fringes creating pale covert bars. Pale supercilium contrasting with dark lores and eye-stripe diagnostic. Crown to back rather plain; thin dark moustachial stripe and fine lateral throat-stripe. Underparts off-white, breast and flanks buff. Legs and bill pinkish grey. Juvenile similar but heavily streaked on back and breast. Call a sparrow-like *tshilp*. Hunts on ground with wagtail-like short runs, pauses and walks. Prefers dry, open rocky or sandy habitats. Widespread but scarce, thinly distributed summer visitor, the only commonly breeding pipit in Greece.

TREE PIPIT *Anthus trivialis* 15cm

Graceful pipit, similar to Meadow Pipit but with a pale supercilium and broad buff-white sub-moustachial stripe. Upperparts warm mid-brown with dark streaks down back; wing feathers dark-centred with pale buff fringes appearing as bars. Underparts whitish with plain yellow-buff to throat and flanks. Legs and bill base pinkish. Call a loud, buzzing *skeeze*; song a variety of trills. Often pumps tail. Hunts on ground but readily flies into trees. Hovering, parachuting songflight characteristic. Favours montane woodlands. Scarce but localised summer visitor to mainland; common and more widespread passage migrant.

MEADOW PIPIT *Anthus pratensis* 14–15cm

Very similar to Tree Pipit, but confusion possible only during migration, when both occur. Winter adult has olive-brown upperparts, dark streaking to back and crown, and dark-centred wing feathers with pale fringes forming two wing-bars. Face rather plain, supercilium inconspicuous. Underparts whitish, breast and flanks warm buff with bold streaking. Bill rather slighter than in Tree Pipit, bill base and legs pinkish. Hindclaw very long. Call, often combined with jerky flight, a thin, squeaky *ist ist ut*. Occurs at ground level in open habitats with short, sparse vegetation, often in flocks. Winter visitor; the commonest and most widespread pipit in Greece.

RED-THROATED PIPIT *Anthus cervinus* 15cm

Similar to Meadow Pipit, but only first-winter birds should cause confusion. Summer male has mid-brown upperparts, boldly streaked dark throughout; wing feathers dark-centred with almost white outer edges, forming two obvious wing-bars. Rusty red on plain face extends to throat and upper breast. Underparts white with heavy flank and breast streaks. Legs pink, bill with yellow base. Winter adult and summer female duller, with more restricted red-buff wash. Juvenile and first-winter lack red and have a white supercilium, throat and underparts, and dark streaking on breast and flanks. Upperparts as in adult but with two white mantle stripes. Call a short, piercing, rather explosive *pssih*. Frequents open habitats with sparse, low vegetation, often in flocks. Uncommon and widespread passage migrant; scarce winter visitor to south.

▲ Winter plumage

WATER PIPIT *Anthus spinoletta* 17–18cm

Robust pipit, the largest in Greece. Summer adult distinctive, with plain ash-grey head, nape and back, and striking white supercilium. Upperparts brown, with paler fringes forming two prominent wing-bars. Underparts plain whitish with pink flush to throat and upper breast. Bill fine and dark, legs black. In flight, white to outer tail obvious. Winter adult upperparts and head brown with buff-white supercilium and throat. Underparts whitish with dark streaks to upper and lower breast and flanks. Call an abrupt *pssit*; song a Meadow Pipit-like trill. Frequents high-altitude slopes and fields in summer, and lowland wetlands and marshes in winter. Scarce local resident in the north; uncommon and widespread winter visitor throughout.

YELLOW WAGTAIL *Motacilla flava* 17cm

Smallest of the four wagtails in Greece, with a shorter tail. Black-headed Wagtail (*M. flava feldegg*) is commonest subspecies; others, including Blue-headed (*M. f. flava*) and Grey-headed (*M. f. thunbergi*), are also recorded on migration. Male Black-headed has olive-brown upperparts and tail, with paler fringes to blackish wing feathers forming two wing-bars. Outer-tail feathers white. Hood black, bill fine and dark. Underparts lemon yellow, legs black. Blue-headed has ashy-blue head with a white supercilium. Grey-headed has a grey-blue hood. Females of all races similar but duller and less contrasting, with a whiter throat and upper breast. Immatures of all races duller brown but retain olive tone to back and pale yellow in vent. Frequents coastal marshes, rice-fields, wet meadows and fields with grazing animals. Common and widespread summer visitor and passage migrant, particularly numerous in autumn.

▼ Feldegg male   ▼ Flava male

▲ Adult male

▲ Juvenile

CITRINE WAGTAIL *Motacilla citreola* 17cm

Slimline wagtail. Summer male has slate-grey upperparts contrasting with white double wing-bar created by white covert fringes and long white tertial edges. Head and underparts yellow, contrasting with slate-grey back. Bill and legs black. Female and winter adult resemble female Yellow Wagtail, but with dusky-grey back and pale yellow cheek surround. Juvenile and first-winter resemble young White Wagtail but with pale supercilium, lores and cheek surround (framing grey cheek), no dark breast-band. Call a rasping *sreep* or *tslie*. Prefers wetland margins and saltmarshes. Widespread though scarce passage migrant.

GREY WAGTAIL *Motacilla cinerea* 18–19cm

Large, slender wagtail with a long tail, which it often pumps up and down. Summer male has grey upperparts, black wing feathers and white-edged dark tertials. Head grey with a black bib, and white supercilium and sub-moustachial stripe. Underparts pale lemon yellow and rump green-yellow. Summer female similar but black bib diffuse or white. Winter adult has a white bib. Juvenile lacks black bib, underparts whitish with a rose-pink tinge and yellow confined to vent. Call a *zi-zi*, sharper than that of White Wagtail. Usually associated with rivers and streams; also found in urban and coastal habitats in winter. Breeds in hills and mountains throughout mainland; scarcer on islands. Fairly common and widespread resident and winter visitor.

▼ Adult male

▼ Adult female

WHITE WAGTAIL *Motacilla alba* 18cm

Slender black-and-white wagtail that constantly pumps tail. Summer
male upperparts pale grey; black wing feathers edged white, making a
double wing-bar. Face white, hindcrown and nape black with distinct
border against grey mantle and back. Throat and upper breast with neat
black bib. Underparts white. Bill and legs dark. Summer female has more
diffuse grey-and-black border at mantle. Winter adult has paler grey head
and upperparts, and no obvious contrast on mantle and nape. Face
white with grey ear-coverts, throat white with black breast-band and
neck-side crescent. Juvenile diffuse grey, duskier. Call an uplifting
tschizzik. Breeds on open rocky coastal and inland wetlands and human-
created habitats. Forms large roosts in reedbeds and towns in winter.
Fairly widespread, scarce resident; common, widespread winter visitor.

WHITE-THROATED DIPPER *Cinclus cinclus* 18cm

Rotund waterside bird with a deep chest and belly, short wings and a
stout, upright tail. Adult distinctive chocolate brown throughout, with a
white throat and upper breast-patch. Bill fine and dark, legs dark and
long. Juvenile cooler brown with pale fringes to upperparts; underparts
dusky whitish, very mottled and scaly. Call a short *zit*; song a more
complex, wavering warble. Sedentary; prefers hill and mountain terrains
with fast rivers and streams. Often observed 'body-bobbing' along river
fringes. Flight straight, fast and low. Widespread but scarce resident,
patchily distributed over much of mainland, scarcer further south.

WINTER WREN *Troglodytes troglodytes* 9–10cm

Tiny, lively bird with a short cocked tail. Upperparts rich brown with dark bars on wings. Face with prominent buff-cream supercilium and medium-length, slightly decurved bill. Underparts paler cream-brown with dark bars, appearing mottled throughout. Loud, rattling *zerrrr* when alarmed; song a beautiful mix of metallic trills and warbles. Often skulks low in scrub and dense cover. Frequents a variety of habitats, from woodland to gardens and hedgerows, usually in more hilly regions. Fairly common and widespread resident, more so on mainland. More common in winter following arrivals from the north.

DUNNOCK *Prunella modularis* 14–15cm

Drab, sparrow-like bird, with a jerky, nervous disposition. Adult has a greyish head and breast, brown ear-coverts, rich brown upperparts with dark streaking and paler brown underparts with reddish-brown streaking, stronger along flanks. Bill thin and dark bill, legs pinkish brown. Juvenile similar but with dense streaks throughout. Song a loud, short, even warble. Breeding mainly restricted to north mainland, in mountainous forests and on open slopes with scattered dense scrub. In winter, occurs throughout in a wide range of habitats, from sea-level upwards. Scarce and local resident; common and widespread winter visitor.

ALPINE ACCENTOR *Prunella collaris* 18cm

Similar to Dunnock but more colourful, larger, bulkier and often more confident. Upperparts grey-brown with dark streaking; wing-coverts black with white tips. Head grey with fine white eye-ring and speckling to paler throat. Underparts paler brown with reddish-brown streaks to flanks. Bill small and dark, with a yellow base. Call a *chak* or rolling *tschirr*; song long, with trills and squeaks. Found in mountains, generally above 2,000m, on rocky slopes with sparse vegetation. Descends to lower altitudes in winter, often congregating around human habitation. In Crete, roosts together in caves, even during the breeding season. Fairly widespread but scarce resident.

RUFOUS-TAILED SCRUB ROBIN *Cercotrichas galactotes* 15cm

Charismatic bird, not unlike Common Nightingale but with a long tail. Cool brown above with buff fringes to brown flight feathers. Crown cool brown, lores and eye-stripe black, supercilium and dark-bordered ear-coverts buff. Rump and outer tail bright rufous chestnut. In flight, tail has jet-black and white tips, central tail feathers cool brown. Underparts buff white. Legs long and pinkish. Call a short tongue-click or whistle; song beautiful and varied. Has a 'butterfly' display flight; perches with tail fanned or cocked high. Breeds in dry, open lowland areas with rocky terrain and sparse scrub; otherwise often seen around dry riverbeds and human habitation. Widespread but scarce summer visitor.

▼ *Adult*

▼ *Adult*

EUROPEAN ROBIN *Erithacus rubecula* 14cm

Very familiar rounded chat with a small dark bill, beady black eye and long, slim brown legs. Adult has mid-brown upperparts and tail, separated from bright orange face, throat and breast by grey tones; underparts whitish. Juvenile brown with extensive scaling. Stance often upright, with wings drooped, head tilted and tail raised. Hops on ground and perches in low vegetation. Call a short *tic*; song a sweet, varied warble. Breeds throughout mainland Greece and some islands. Scarcer in south, nesting in fir and mixed woodland at altitude; commoner in a variety of habitats and altitudes in north. Fairly common and widespread resident; very common winter visitor, when numbers are swelled by arrivals from the north.

COMMON NIGHTINGALE *Luscinia megarhynchos* 16–17cm

Shy, secretive chat with plain brown plumage, upright stance, long legs and often cocked tail. Similar to European Robin but larger, longer-tailed and plain. Adult upperparts warm brown with rufous brown to rump and uppertail. Underparts dull, creamy brown, paler on throat and vent. Face plain with pale eye-ring. Juvenile similar but very scaly throughout. Known for its beautiful, liquid song in early spring; alarm call a grating *krrr*. Prefers dry woodland and scrub with dense undergrowth, hillsides and large gardens, often near human habitation. Common and widespread summer visitor.

BLACK REDSTART *Phoenicurus ochruros* 14–15cm

Smart, upright chat. Male has dark grey upperparts, paler grey underparts, and black face and breast. Note white wing-panel and rich chestnut tail and rump. Fine bill and legs black. Female and juvenile duller, more uniform grey-brown, but retain chestnut rump and tail. Readily quivers tail. Prefers open rocky areas with scattered scrub, often around buildings and human habitation. Breeds over much of mainland, often above treeline. Winters more frequently in lowland areas. Fairly widespread, locally common resident; common and widespread winter visitor, when population is boosted by arrivals from the north.

COMMON REDSTART *Phoenicurus phoenicurus* 14cm

Small, upright, tail-quivering chat, slighter than Black Redstart. Male striking, with dark grey-brown upperparts, jet-black face and throat, and white forehead. Underparts orange, whiter from belly to tail. Uppertail and rump chestnut. Female similar to Black Redstart female, but brown replaced by grey and more chestnut on rump. Juvenile brown and scaly. First-winter male like female, but throat speckled black and breast a stronger orange. Arboreal, breeding in open woodland. Scarce and local summer visitor; common passage migrant. Less common than Black Redstart, with breeding range restricted to north mainland. Widespread across mainland and islands during migration. Western population is nominate race; eastern race is *P. p. samamisicus*, male with a white wing-panel.

▼ *Adult male* ▼ *Adult female*

WHINCHAT *Saxicola rubetra* 12–13cm

Compact, sturdy chat, most similar to European Stonechat; whitish supercilium is key to identification. Male has dark brown-black head with prominent white supercilium. Upperparts patterned mid-brown and black. Wings blackish with white wing-panel. Underparts orange from throat through breast, fading to white on belly and vent. Rump with yellow-brown and black spots. Tail black with white base, obvious in flight. Female similar, but with buff supercilium, paler brown head and upperparts, and softer apricot underparts; lacks white wing-panel. Juvenile like female but with white spots on back. Prefers meadows and open grassland habitats; often perches upright on grass stems or bushes. Breeding confined to mountainous treeline habitats. Scarce and local summer visitor; common passage migrant.

EUROPEAN STONECHAT *Saxicola rubicola* 12–13cm

Boldly marked chat; only confusion species is Whinchat. Male striking, with black head, partial white neck collar, dark brown upperparts with white shoulder-patch and white rump. Upper breast burnt orange, fading to paler tones towards belly. Female more like female Whinchat, with streaky brown head and upperparts, paler orange underparts, and a warm brown rump-patch with dark brown spots. White wing-panel also present. Juvenile shows hint of white wing-panel and retains brown rump-patch, but otherwise pale brown with dark streaks. Agitated call a repeated *vizt-tak-tak*. Frequents open areas with low vegetation, from mountains to coasts. Common and widespread resident.

▼ *Adult male*   ▼ *Adult female*

▲ Adult

▲ Immature female

ISABELLINE WHEATEAR *Oenanthe isabellina* 16–17cm

Pale, upright wheatear. Summer adult has uniform taupe upperparts with a conspicuous dark alula on pale brown wings. Prominent white supercilium, fore-supercilium and throat contrast with black lores (browner on female). Pale buff from cheeks to flanks, white from lower breast to undertail. In all ages, tail has black terminal band and black central feathers rising into white tail base and rump. Juvenile more buff throughout, with less obvious face pattern and scaling to breast. Ground-dwelling, hopping and running for insects; perches in the open. Frequents dry, open, rocky hillsides, usually near coasts; found in a variety of habitats during spring passage, even suburban Athens! Rare local summer visitor, restricted to northern mainland and a couple of Aegean islands; scarce, widespread passage migrant, particularly in spring.

NORTHERN WHEATEAR *Oenanthe oenanthe* 14–16cm

Slender chat with upright stance, and dark legs and wings. Male striking, with slate-grey crown and back, black wings and eye-mask, and white supercilium and fore-supercilium. Underparts apricot-buff and white. In all ages, tail has black terminal band and black central feathers rising into white tail base and white rump. In winter male, grey upperparts replaced by taupe but retains black eye-mask and wings, the latter with pale feather fringes. Female with brown-grey back and contrasting darker brown wings. Lores and ear-coverts brown, supercilium mostly buff with some white. Juvenile brown, very scaly. Often perches on exposed rocks; runs and hops for ground insects. Prefers open rocky habitats, grassland and sand dunes. Common and widespread summer visitor and passage migrant.

▼ Adult male

▼ Adult female

BLACK-EARED WHEATEAR *Oenanthe hispanica* 14.5cm

Smaller than Isabelline and Northern Wheatears. Summer male very distinctive, with black face and wings on otherwise uniform white plumage with faint apricot-brown tones (can have a pale apricot throat). Summer female has dark brown face and wings. contrasting with paler orangey-brown back, crown and upper breast. Underparts warm white. In all ages, has a white rump and tail, the latter with narrow black terminal band and sides, and black central feathers extending into white base. Winter male brown with less extensive black on face and pale-edged dark wings. Call a familiar *chak*; song rather buoyant, explosive, variable. Common in open rocky areas with low scrub. Common and widespread summer visitor.

COMMON ROCK THRUSH *Monticola saxatilis* 18–19cm

Large, robust chat-like thrush with a strong bill and legs, and stubby tail. Male stunning, with blue-grey head and rump, conspicuous white patch on back, mid-brown wings and russet-orange underparts and tail, the latter with brown central feathers. Female retains tail pattern and colour, but plumage otherwise dark brown above with pale feather fringes, and orange-brown below with dark barring. Juvenile similar to female but with more densely dark scaling to underparts. Prefers rocky scree and stony hillsides with scattered vegetation, and lowland habitats on spring passage. Fairly common and widespread summer visitor and passage migrant to mountains of mainland Greece; absent from most islands.

BLUE ROCK THRUSH *Monticola solitarius* 20cm

Slightly bigger than Common Rock Thrush, with longer bill and tail. Male distinctive, with dusky-blue plumage throughout and blackish wings and tail. In poor light can appear all black like Common Blackbird, but distinguished by smaller size, larger dark bill and dark legs. Female dark brown on upperparts, lighter brown with pale scaling and dark barring on underparts. Notably more heavily patterned and colder brown than female Common Blackbird. Juvenile resembles female but with paler scaling to upperparts. Inhabits rocky outcrops, gorges and old buildings, usually from sea-level to around 1,000m. Fairly common and widespread resident, although thinly distributed.

COMMON BLACKBIRD *Turdus merula* 24–25cm

Familiar medium-sized thrush with a rounded head and long tail, often jerked upwards with wings dropped. Male black above and below, with a thin yellow eye-ring and yellow bill. First-winter male has all-dark bill and eye-ring, and brown plumage contrasting with darker wings. Female mid-brown throughout with brown-speckled whitish throat and breast. Bill dull yellow. Juvenile brown with paler buff speckling throughout and more uniform mid-brown wings. Call often a loud *chook*; song a rich, fluty warble. Found in a variety of habitats, from hillside woodlands to farmland, parks, gardens and buildings. Common and widespread resident.

▼ *Adult male*　　　　　　　　▼ *Adult female*

FIELDFARE *Turdus pilaris* 25–26cm

Robust, colourful long-tailed thrush. Head and nape grey with chestnut-brown back and wings, pale grey rump and all-dark tail. Restricted white supercilium, smudgy black lores and dark-tipped yellow-based bill. Chin creamy yellow, throat and breast with dark spotting and streaks that continue along flanks. Belly and vent white. In flight, grey rump, dark tail and whitish underwing very obvious. Call a distinctive, loud *shack-shack-shack*, heard in flight. Prefers open woodland, countryside, orchards and rough farmland. Fairly common and widespread winter visitor, most frequent in north mainland, often forming large roaming flocks.

SONG THRUSH *Turdus philomelos* 23cm

Smaller than similar Mistle Thrush, with rounder shape and shorter tail. Upperparts warm brown. Head brown buff with darker brown ear-coverts and gloss stripe, and pale buff lores and eye-ring. Underparts white with yellow-buff wash to breast and brown spotting throughout. Bill small and dark with yellowish base, legs pale pink. Call a high, clipped *sip*, often heard in flight; song beautiful, fluty and repetitive, often from treetops. Favours woodland, farmland, orchards and gardens, and often abundant in olive groves. Breeding limited to mainly northern woodlands at mid- to high altitudes. Scarce local resident; very common, widespread winter visitor.

REDWING *Turdus iliacus* 21cm

Size of a Song Thrush but with a pale cream supercilium and sub-moustachial stripe, black lores and rusty-red flank patches. Upperparts warm brown; underparts whitish with brown streaks and spots to chin, throat, breast and flanks. Bill black with yellow base, legs pink. Underwing dusky cream with dark red-brown coverts (paler orange-brown in Song Thrush). Call a high-pitched, thin *seeep*. Found in open woodland, countryside, farmland and gardens. Fairly common and widespread winter visitor, arriving in large flocks in late autumn. Like Song Thrush, targeted by hunters in winter.

MISTLE THRUSH *Turdus viscivorus* 27cm

Sturdy thrush with long wings and tail, and a bold upright stance. At a distance, looks long-bodied and pot-bellied. Upperparts cold grey-brown with pale-edged wing feathers. Face whitish with dark brown crescent around ear-coverts. Underparts white, often darker on breast-sides, all with dark brown spots, these finer and more streaked around neck. White underwing-coverts and outer tail notable in flight, which is undulating and powerful. Distinctive rattling call, often in flight; song rather mournful. Prefers coniferous woodland from 500m to the treeline; scarce in lowlands in winter compared to other thrushes. Fairly common and widespread resident, commoner on mainland.

CETTI'S WARBLER *Cettia cetti* 13–14cm

Medium-sized brown warbler, with short wings and a long rounded tail. Not unlike Winter Wren in skulking nature, coloration and posture; often raises, fans and regularly flicks tail. Upperparts rufous brown, underparts paler greyish brown. Head with often slightly raised rufous-brown crown; indistinct white supercilium and throat contrast with dark lores and eye-stripe. More likely to be heard than seen. Call a harsh *chip*; song loud, short and explosive. Prefers lowland wetlands or damp habitats with dense, low vegetation. Fairly common and widespread resident.

ZITTING CISTICOLA *Cisticola juncidis* 10cm

Very small warbler, with a short, broad tail. Distinctive, with a compact body, short wings and tail, and buoyant, undulating songflight. Upperparts sandy brown with darker brown streaking down back, rump and crown (the latter more solid brown in summer male). Wings brown with pale fringes to feathers. Face pale brown-buff with a slightly decurved bill, dark in male, pink in female. Throat and underparts whitish with gingery buff to breast and flanks. In flight, uppertail shows white and black to tips. Call a loud *chipp*; song sharp, repetitive *zip-zip-zip-zip*. Prefers coastal wetlands and marshes with tall vegetation. Fairly common and widespread resident of coastal mainland and some islands.

SAVI'S WARBLER *Locustella luscinioides* 14cm

Plain, sturdy brown warbler with a long, broad tail. Good views needed to separate it from the rarer passage Common Grasshopper and River warblers (*L. naevia* and *L. fluviatilis*; not illustrated), and Marsh and Eurasian Reed warbler. Upperparts uniform rich brown; rather curved wings have thin white outer edge to leading primary feather. Long, dusky-buff undertail-coverts show conspicuous paler feather tips. Face with pale supercilium, throat whitish. Underparts whitish with brown-buff to upper breast and flanks. Call a sharp, loud *pvitt*; song a diagnostic, endless reeling, like a loud insect, often at night. Strongly associated with reedbeds. Scarce local summer visitor; fairly uncommon and widespread passage migrant. Breeds in scattered wetlands in north mainland.

MOUSTACHED WARBLER *Acrocephalus melanopogon* 12–13cm

Neat warbler with well-rounded features and a broad tail, like Sedge Warbler. Strong head pattern aids identification: blackish crown, broad-ended white supercilium and white throat, blackish eye-stripe, dusky ear-coverts and hint of a dark moustachial stripe. Upperparts warm brown with darker streaks along back, appearing uniform at distance. Underparts warm buff, white at belly and undertail. Longish legs and bill dark. Call a *tuck* or louder, rolling *trrrt*, diagnostic in winter reedbeds; song complex and repetitive, like that of Eurasian Reed Warbler. Favours coastal habitats with reedbeds (often seen foraging at edges), marshes, and drier marginal areas with bushes. Rare local resident in north; fairly common winter visitor, the only *Acrocephalus* warbler to overwinter in Greece.

SEDGE WARBLER *Acrocephalus schoenobaenus* 13cm

More slender-bodied and paler than similar Moustached Warbler, with a rounded tail. Upperparts mid-brown, clearly streaked dark brown on crown, nape and back. Rump unmarked rufous brown. Wing feathers with dark centres and paler edges. Face with buff-cream supercilium and dusky-brown ear-coverts. Throat whitish, underparts cream to warm buff, unmarked, though hint of breast streaking in immature birds. Call a sharp, rolling *errrr*; song long, excitable, with trills, whistles, squeaks and grating, sometimes also mimics. Associated with reedbeds and marshes, and drier marginal wetlands with bushes and scrub. Scarce local summer visitor; common passage migrant, occurring in good numbers. Breeding appears to be restricted to northern areas.

EURASIAN REED WARBLER *Acrocephalus scirpaceus* 13cm

Plain, skulking warbler with a peaked crown, flat forehead, slim bill and rounded tail. Significantly smaller than Great Reed Warbler. Very similar to Marsh Warbler – some silent, worn adults and juveniles cannot be separated in the field. Adult dull brown above with subtly warmer chestnut-brown rump. Whitish buff below, strongest along flanks. Face with pale buff supercilium only at front of eye, lores dark. Legs dark brownish pink. In autumn, greyer brown, duller and worn, with more white below. Juvenile shows more chestnut brown to upperparts and extensive buff below. Call often a rolling *churr churr*; song long, repetitive, churring, whistling, grating *kerr-kerr-kerr chiri chiri chiri* or similar, delivered in low, guttural pitches. Associated strongly with reedbeds. Common and widespread summer visitor and passage migrant.

▲ Adult male ▲ Adult female

MARSH WARBLER *Acrocephalus palustris* 13cm

Very similar to Eurasian Reed and Great Reed Warblers, but scarcer in summer and less numerous on migration. Upperparts more olive-toned throughout, without the warmer rump of Eurasian Reed and with longer wings. Wing shows pale edging to tertials and tips of primaries. Legs yellowish pink. Autumn birds harder to differentiate, but overall paler, colder brown with creamy flanks, lacking warm tones of Eurasian Reed. Call a distinctive *chuc*; song less repetitive than Eurasian Reed's, with more varied chattering and warbling, and some mimicry. Prefers bushes and low, dense vegetation along wetland fringes. Scarce local summer visitor to northern wetlands; fairly common passage migrant throughout, particularly in autumn.

GREAT REED WARBLER *Acrocephalus arundinaceus* 19–20cm

Easy to identify, being robust and heavy, nearly double the size of Eurasian Reed Warbler, and with a proportionately larger bill and peaked head. Upperparts cold to mid-brown, wings long and tail rounded. Head with pink-based dark bill, obvious buff supercilium, dark lores and eye-stripe, and white throat. Underparts whitish with warm buff to breast-sides and flanks. Legs sturdy and dark. Juvenile warmer brown throughout. Song similar but coarser than that of Eurasian Reed. Frequents same habitats as Eurasian Reed, favouring large reedbeds. Common and widespread summer visitor and passage migrant.

▼ Adult male ▼ Adult female

EASTERN OLIVACEOUS WARBLER *Iduna pallida* 12–14cm

Plain, washed-out warbler, not unlike a tea-coloured Eurasian Reed Warbler. Upperparts tea grey to olive green-brown, tail square-ended. Underparts whitish with dull greyish breast-sides and flanks. Head with rather flat forehead, pale supercilium and eye-ring, and mid-brown lores. Bill long, thin and pointed; lower mandible pink, upper grey. Greyish rump and pale grey outer edges to wing feathers aid separation from Eurasian Reed; like that species, dips and raises tail. Call a *tack*; song comprises long, low notes and squeaky high ones in warbling repetition. Prefers dry open areas, orchards, parks and gardens, and riverside vegetation. Common, widespread summer visitor from late April.

OLIVE-TREE WARBLER *Hippolais olivetorum* 24–26cm

Very large, bulky grey warbler with a stout bill, long wings and sturdy legs. Upperparts mid-grey, obviously blackish tail and outer wing contrasting with whitish-edged tertials and secondaries, giving the effect of a pale panel. Head grey with angled forehead, pale supercilium, fine eye-ring and whitish throat. Bill with dull yellow lower mandible, grey upper. Underparts dull white with greyish wash to breast and flanks. Legs dark grey. Call a deep *chack* or *tak*; song quite distinctive and complex, long, slow and deep, with a rich guttural quality. Inhabits olive groves, scrubland, orchards, open woodland and parkland in lowlands and on hillsides, often near coasts. Fairly common and widespread summer visitor.

▲ *Immature autumn*

ICTERINE WARBLER *Hippolais icterina* 13–14cm

A striking warbler with lemon-yellow tones, unlike any other regular migrant warbler in Greece. Upperparts greyish green; wings long, feathers brown-centred with whitish edges on tertials and secondaries forming a pale panel, most notable in spring. Head grey-green, often with angled hindcrown, yellow lores and small dark eye. Bill pale with yellowish-pink base. Underparts with lemon-yellow wash, whitish towards belly. Legs grey. In autumn, upperparts greyer and worn, underparts with reduced yellow and more white. Prefer thickets, dense low vegetation and copses near water. Fairly common and widespread passage migrant.

EURASIAN BLACKCAP *Sylvia atricapilla* 13cm

Sturdy warbler. Male has uniform grey-brown upperparts and paler grey underparts. Grey head has a distinct black cap reaching down to eye, and at close range shows dark eyes with lower white eye crescent. Lacks white in tail. Legs and bill grey. Female similar but cap chestnut brown. Juvenile has a blackish cap that in females wears away during first winter to reveal brown. Call a hard *tack*, similar to that of Lesser Whitethroat; song fluty, chattering, beautifully melodious, often heard echoing through woodlands in spring. Found in woodland with dense understorey, along vegetated riverbanks, on hillsides, and in ravines, parks and gardens. Common and widespread resident throughout Greece; common passage migrant and winter visitor.

▼ *Adult male*   ▼ *Adult female*

GARDEN WARBLER *Sylvia borin* 14cm

Very plain, rather featureless warbler. Upperparts pale grey-brown, underparts paler beige-white. Face grey-brown, with an 'open' expression and obvious black eye. Sturdy bill and legs grey. Lacks white in tail. First-winter can show obvious pale fringes to tertials. Call an irritated, repeated *vik*; song beautiful, sweet, long and fast, similar to Eurasian Blackcap's but slightly harsher. Favours scrub, moist woodland, parks, gardens and riverside undergrowth. Rare local summer visitor in north mainland, fairly common passage migrant.

BARRED WARBLER *Sylvia nisoria* 15–16cm

Robust, long-tailed warbler. Male striking, plumage resembling Common Cuckoo's. Upperparts and head storm grey, eye a contrasting yellow. Wings dark brown, with white covert tips forming bars, and underparts white with brown barring throughout. In all ages, shows white tips to tail, obvious in flight. Female a muted version of male, with browner-grey upperparts, dull yellow eye and brown chevrons (not bars) on buff-white underparts. First-winter birds in autumn have pale grey-brown upperparts and head, pale grey-buff underparts. Wing and uppertail have pale edges to feathers, giving a scaled appearance and in wing forming two pale bars. Undertail-coverts whitish with conspicuous dark chevrons throughout, sometimes extending onto flanks. Favours scrub and scattered trees in open countryside. Rare local summer visitor to north mainland; scarce passage migrant throughout, mainly in autumn.

▼ *Adult male*

▼ *Immature autumn*

LESSER WHITETHROAT *Sylvia curruca* 12–14cm

Small, compact warbler with rounded features and a fairly short tail. Upperparts uniform earth brown. Head storm grey with darker ear-coverts and white crescent around base of eye. Fine bill and legs dark. Throat white, underparts whitish cream with a warm buff wash to flanks. Undertail unmarked, white. Autumn birds can look very worn and greyer on upperparts. Call a low *tuk* or *trrrrr*; song a repetitive loud rattling and trilling. Prefers scrubby mountainous habitats and mixed woodlands. Fairly common but local summer visitor, biased towards mountains of north and central mainland, and with some very localised island breeding; locally common passage migrant to mainly north-east mainland and northern Aegean islands.

COMMON WHITETHROAT *Sylvia communis* 14cm

Similar to Lesser Whitethroat, but larger, longer-tailed and with more complex plumage. Male has earth-brown upperparts with chestnut brown to outer fringes of dark wing feathers. Head uniform mid-grey through crown and ear-coverts, with white eye-ring and pink bill base. Throat white, upper breast and flanks buff-white with variable pink tinge. Legs pink. Female and first-year male upperparts and head much browner and duller, lacking grey but retaining contrasting chestnut wings and white throat. Bill browner and duller, ear-coverts warm brown. Call a *tak* or irritated *churr*; song a rather jumbled, lively warble. Prefers scrubby areas, dense bushes, hedgerows, woodland fringes and farmland. Common and widespread summer visitor and passage migrant, the commonest *Sylvia* warbler during migration.

EASTERN ORPHEAN WARBLER *Sylvia crassirostris* 15cm

Large, robust warbler, rather like Barred Warbler in structure and Lesser Whitethroat in plumage. Summer male smart, with mid-grey upperparts, dark smoky-grey head, distinct pale eye and neat white throat. Underparts white with variable pinkish wash to breast and flanks. Undertail-coverts pale with light brown chevrons. Legs and bill dark. Tail long and square-ended with white outer feathers. Female and immature lighter on head and more diffuse grey-brown, with dark smoky-grey only on ear-coverts and lores, very like an oversized Lesser Whitethroat. Upperparts browner grey and eye colour variable (dark in juvenile). Prefers tall vegetation, scrub, hedgerows, olive groves and woodland with dense understorey. Widespread but scarce summer visitor.

SUBALPINE WARBLER *Sylvia cantillans* 12cm

Rather slim warbler with a short, fine bill and short tail. Male has blue-grey upperparts, blackish wings with white fringes to feathers, beautiful blue-grey head, red eye-ring, brick-red throat and broad white moustachial stripe. Underparts brick red on breast, otherwise white, with faint pinkish-buff wash to flanks. In flight, white on outer tail obvious. Female duller brown-grey above, with a grey head, white eye-ring, less conspicuous white moustachial stripe and pinkish-tinged white throat. Juvenile pale brown above and on head, with chestnut fringes to dark-centred wing feathers. Call a *chak*; song a long, rattling, fluty musical mix. Prefers dry, open countryside and hillsides with plentiful bush understorey. Common and widespread summer visitor, more frequent in north.

SARDINIAN WARBLER *Sylvia melanocephala* 13–14cm
. . . .
Large-headed, long-tailed, slender warbler with a peaked forehead. Male distinctive, its black head and large red eye-ring contrasting with white throat. Upperparts storm grey, darker on wings. Underparts dusky grey throughout flanks, whiter on belly and undertail. In flight, shows broad white tips to tail and white outer tail. Female and juvenile have grey head, white throat and red eye-ring. Upperparts warm brown with dark centres to wing feathers. Underparts warm brown, colour stronger along flanks. Similar to female Subalpine Warbler, but darker plumage and red eye-ring distinctive. Call a rattling *kre kre krekrekre*; song a long mix of hard, fast warbles, chatters and rattles. Frequents dry countryside, open woodland with dense understorey, dry coastal scrub and gardens. Common and widespread resident.

RÜPPELL'S WARBLER *Sylvia ruppeli* 14cm
. . . .
Endemic to the Mediterranean. Male distinctive, with a black forecrown, face and throat separated by a white moustachial stripe. Eye-ring red, upperparts and back of head dark grey, wings blackish with conspicu-ous white fringes to feathers. Underparts smoky grey throughout. Tail blackish with white outer-tail feathers. Female duller brown-grey above, dark grey on head, and throat clean white or with variable black spotting. Juvenile browner throughout, with white throat and only a hint of moustachial stripe, if any. Both female and juvenile have subtle brownish-white eye-ring. Call and song like those of Sardinian Warbler, often from top of tall bush or during airborne parachute display. Frequents dry rocky slopes, mountains and hillsides with dense, often thorny scrub. Fairly widespread, locally common summer visitor, with a strong southern mainland and island bias.

EASTERN BONELLI'S WARBLER *Phylloscopus orientalis* 11–12cm

Small, pale, plain-faced leaf warbler. Crown, nape and back pale grey. Wings, rump and tail bright green-yellow. In spring, variable worn whitish fringes on greater coverts and tertials create a pale panel. Small peppercorn-like black eye, 'open' whitish face, grey lores, and buff supercilium and ear-coverts. Throat and underparts uniform white. Bill small with a pink base, legs grey. Call a *chup*; song a repetitive, high-pitched *sve*, not unlike that of Wood Warbler. Favours open pine and oak woodland at altitude. Fairly widespread and locally fairly common summer visitor and passage migrant. Breeding distribution biased towards north mainland.

WOOD WARBLER *Phylloscopus sibilatrix* 12cm

Stockiest of the regular *Phylloscopus* warblers in Greece, with longer wings, a short tail, stronger bill and strikingly brighter, well-defined plumage. Spring adult has sage-green upperparts with a brighter mossy-green rump and paler yellowy edges to wing feathers. Head, eye-stipe and lores sage green, contrasting with bright yellow supercilium, ear-coverts, throat and upper breast-sides. Underparts gleaming white throughout. Autumn adult and juvenile similar but with pale-edged tertials and primary tips, and duller yellow upperparts. Readily hovers while feeding in canopy. Prefers moist deciduous woodland. Call a sharp *zip*; song a distinctive reeling trill. Rare local summer visitor, with a small population on the northern mainland border; common passage migrant, particularly in spring.

COMMON CHIFFCHAFF *Phylloscopus collybita* 10–11cm

Rather nondescript brown-and-beige warbler, but a number of features aid identification. Upperparts brown-green. Face weakly patterned with a dark eye, hint of whitish under-eye crescent, brown eye-stripe, and buff-brown supercilium, ear-coverts and throat. Underparts cooler buff-beige with a faint yellow wash along flanks. Legs and small bill almost black, distinctive among *Phylloscopus* warblers. Constantly dips tail when active, unlike Willow Warbler. Call a fine, soft *hweet*; song a familiar, steady, repetitive *chiff-chaff*. Favours woodland, scrub, gardens and varied lowland habitats. Fairly common but local summer visitor, with a restricted breeding range in wooded mountains of north; common and widespread winter visitor.

WILLOW WARBLER *Phylloscopus trochilus* 10–12cm

Very similar to Common Chiffchaff, but good views should aid identification. Has more striking head pattern, with a stronger, longer supercilium, more obvious eye-stripe and more extensive yellow wash to face, supercilium and underparts (though variable). Legs usually pale pinkish brown. Upperparts usually greyer and cooler, with longer wings giving more elongated shape overall. Juvenile brighter, with extensive yellow on underparts. Call a *hooeet*; distinctive descending song may be heard on spring passage. Found in a variety of woodland, scrub and garden habitats. Widespread and very common passage migrant in Greece, if not the most common, particularly in autumn.

GOLDCREST *Regulus regulus* 9cm

Tiny, rounded, short-tailed bird, rather like a *Phylloscopus* warbler but separable on plumage. Adult upperparts olive green with a striking black wing-patch, double white wing-bar and white-tipped dark tertials. Head grey, eye tiny and black with broad white surround. Crest (readily raised) has black-bordered yellow stripe (brighter orange in male). Underparts dirty white-buff. Juvenile grey-green, plain-headed. Call a repeated high-pitched *zsee*; song a repeated thin trill and twittering, ending with a jangling flourish. In winter, favours lowland habitats, gardens, mixed woodland and scrub. Breeds in coniferous woodland at altitude. Fairly common but localised resident, breeding in central and northern mainland; common and widespread winter visitor in varying numbers.

COMMON FIRECREST *Regulus ignicapilla* 9cm

Similar to Goldcrest but with bolder plumage. Adult upperparts moss green with a black wing-patch and contrasting white wing-bars (as in Goldcrest), and a bright bronzy-yellow collar-patch. Head distinctive, with a broad white supercilium (extends onto orange-washed forehead) and under-eye surround, grey ear-coverts, orange crown-stripe with black borders that join at forehead, and thin black eye-stripe, lores and moustachial stripe. Underparts pale off-white, warmer around throat. Juvenile grey-green, plain but with obvious supercilium. Call and song like Goldcrest's, but song simpler, with repeated *si* notes increasing in volume and intensity. Favours woodland and scrub at altitude; less commonly associated with coniferous woodland than Goldcrest. Fairly common and widespread resident.

SPOTTED FLYCATCHER *Muscicapa striata* 14–15cm

Rather plain, slender, long-winged flycatcher with an upright stance. Adult upperparts greyish, wings darker grey with white feather fringes. Head grey with dark streaking through crown. Throat and underparts off-white with subtle streaking across breast. Legs and bill dark. Juvenile similar but with pale spots to upperparts. Perches in open. Call a short, high *zee*; song a mix of simple, scratchy, squeaky notes and trills. Frequents open woodland, orchards, gardens and olive groves. Widespread and locally common summer visitor; common passage migrant, particularly in autumn. The commonest flycatcher in Greece.

SEMICOLLARED FLYCATCHER *Ficedula semitorquata* 13cm

Very like Collared and Pied flycatchers. Male has a white half neck collar, more extensive than in Pied but not full as in Collared. Large white patch in wing, with additional 'finger' bar of white extending across median coverts (not seen in males of the other species). White primary bar broad (even larger in Collared), and has white in tail (absent in Collared Flycatcher and less extensive in Pied). Female grey above, with less extensive white on wing than female Collared and Pied, and white primary patch a reduced bar near wing edge. Call a *tsrr*; song soft and whistling. Favours woodlands at altitude in north. Nests in old wood-pecker holes. Fairly common local summer visitor; widespread passage migrant, particularly in spring.

COLLARED FLYCATCHER *Ficedula albicollis* 13cm

Most like Semicollared Flycatcher (see that species). Male differs in having a full white neck collar, conspicuous white rump-patch and larger white forehead-patch. White wing-patch is large, and white primary bar is conspicuous and broad. Often lacks white in outer tail. Female resembles female Semicollared and Pied flycatchers, and can be indistinguishable in the field. Upperparts greyer than in Pied; wings with broader white primary patch, this nearly reaching wing edge (hardly visible and not to edge in Pied), and an obvious bar rather than a patch in Semicollared). Call a thin whistle. Frequents varied open woodland and countryside habitats. Common and widespread passage migrant.

EUROPEAN PIED FLYCATCHER *Ficedula hypoleuca* 13cm

Compact flycatcher with a rounded belly and short tail that it flicks regularly. Male upperparts black or dark brown (on passage in spring, often chocolate brown) with a small white forehead-patch. Underparts snow white from throat to undertail. Wing black or dark brown with large white wing-patch and smaller white primary bar, the latter sometimes barely visible and not to edge of wing. Tail black, outer tail white. Legs and bill black. Female and first-winter similar but with pale brown upperparts, no white on forehead and reduced wing-patch. Female difficult to separate from female Semicollared and Collared flycatchers. Call a *whit* or *tic*. Common and widespread passage migrant, particularly in spring. The most common of the pied flycatchers. Bird of varied woodland and countryside on migration.

▼ *Spring male*

▼ *Immature female*

 Adult male ▲ *Adult female*

BEARDED REEDLING *Panurus biarmicus* 12–13cm

Beautiful tit-like bird of reedbed habitats, comparable in size to a Great Tit but with a long tail. Both sexes have sandy-brown to yellow upperparts and short black, sandy-brown and white wings. Male particularly striking, with a blue-grey head and broad, tapering, vertical black moustache contrasting with white throat. Tail very long, sandy brown and graduated, undertail-coverts black. Underparts whitish with buff-yellow to sandy wash along breast-sides and flanks. Bill tiny and yellow, legs black. Female has a pale sandy-buff head, off-white throat and whitish undertail. Juvenile resembles female but with black on lores, back and outer tail. Call distinctive, a lively *ping*. Fairly common but local resident of major wetlands, particularly in north and north-west.

MARSH TIT *Poecile palustris* 11–12cm

Small rounded tit, with dull brown upperparts, a glossy black cap and small black bib. Face white, underparts off-white with buff-brown wash to flanks. Call a lively *phicuas* or *pitchew*; song simple, comprising one or two repeated high-pitched ringing notes. Inhabits deciduous woodland. Fairly widespread and locally common resident at medium-low altitudes. Willow Tit (*P. hyrcanus*; not illustrated), a rarer local resident, is very similar but differs subtly in having a matt black cap, larger bib and pale wing-panel. Call a harsh, nasally *tchay tchay* or *chaa chaa*, or *zi* notes. Generally inhabits coniferous woodland in higher northern (Rhodopes) and central mountain ranges, although distribution is still largely unknown.

SOMBRE TIT *Parus lugubris* 14cm

Similar in size to Great Tit but plumage resembles that of smaller Marsh Tit. Differs in cold, grey-toned upperparts and pale grey underparts, some with a warm buff wash to upper breast and flanks. Head has a straight-based brown-black cap above white face, and large blackish throat-patch reaching to upper breast. Call a *si-si-si* or excitable *chrrrt*; song a fast, rather grating *chriv-chriv-chriv*. Frequents a range of habitats, including dry hillsides, open deciduous woodlands, open areas with scattered trees and low dense vegetation, olive groves and orchards, from sea-level to high altitudes. Widespread but scarce resident.

COAL TIT *Periparus ater* 11–12cm

Similar in size to Eurasian Blue Tit, but head larger and tail shorter. More colourful than the other three black-capped tits in Greece. Upperparts blue-grey with two distinct narrow white wings-bars. Head black and white, with black cap and nape broken by conspicuous white nape-patch, a large triangular black bib and white cheek-patches. Dusky pink-buff on flanks to otherwise off-white underparts. Favours coniferous woodland in high mountains, but also found in mixed woodland in the north; more numerous in lowlands in winter as birds filter down from higher altitudes and latitudes. Common and widespread resident.

EURASIAN BLUE TIT *Cyanistes caeruleus* 11–12cm

Very familiar bird with beautiful bright plumage. Only confusion species is Great Tit, but that is much larger. Body round and compact, wings and tail short. Back blue-green, wings blue with white wing-bar, and tail blue. Underparts lemon yellow throughout. Head with blue cap, and slim black eye-stripe and neck collar on white face. Frequents deciduous woodland, olive groves and gardens at low and medium altitudes. Very common and widespread resident, but absent from some dry lowland areas of southern mainland and several islands.

GREAT TIT *Parus major* 14cm

Striking, beautifully bold tit, similar to Eurasian Blue Tit but much larger. Back green, tail and wings blue-grey with obvious white wing-bar. Head glossy black with large white cheek-patch. Underparts lemon yellow throughout, with broad black stripe running from throat to underbelly (stripe narrower and broken in slightly duller female). Calls include a single-note *tink*; song loud, sharp repeated *teacher-teacher*. Favours a variety of habitats, from coniferous woodlands to gardens and olive groves at low and high altitudes. Common, and the most widespread resident tit in Greece (missing from only a few Aegean islands).

LONG-TAILED TIT *Aegithalos caudatus* 14cm (9cm tail)

Unmistakable tiny tit with a very long tail that comprises over half its total length. Upperparts predominantly black, with a black back, rose-pink shoulder, black wings with a pale wing-panel, and black tail with white outer-tail feathers. Head white with a black stripe across face and side of crown, joining black nape. Underparts white with a rose-pink flush to flanks and underbelly. Small bill and legs black. Eye-ring dark pink. Fast and aerobatic, often moving through trees in small parties. Call a loud *zee-zee-zee*, soft *pit* or high trill. Inhabits various woodlands, scrub and gardens. Fairly common and widespread resident, particularly in north. The grey-headed race *A. c. tephronotus* occurs on Lesvos and Samos.

KRÜPER'S NUTHATCH *Sitta krueperi* 12–13cm

Compact nuthatch, with a small head, pointed bill, and short legs and tail. Upperparts grey-blue. Head with a blue-grey crown and black patch to forecrown. White supercilium above narrow black eye-stripe and white cheeks and throat. Underparts dirty white (with blue-grey tones in male); striking orange-russet breast-patch and undertail-coverts, peppered with white chevrons. Call a typical nuthatch *doid*; song comprises repeated fast and slow trills. Has a very horizontal stance, and uses legs to move up and down trunks and branches; very agile in upper canopy. Favours Calabrian Pine (*Pinus brutia*) woodland; nests in pine and Sweet Chestnut (*Castanea sativa*) trees, and in old Middle Spotted Woodpecker holes. Rare local resident, found only on Lesvos.

EURASIAN NUTHATCH *Sitta europaea* 14cm

Medium-sized nuthatch with an almond-shaped body, short tail and large head. Bill spear-like and strong; legs sturdy and positioned far back along often horizontally poised body. Upperparts blue-grey, including crown and tail. Long black eye-stripe with downward curve extends to mantle base. Cheeks white and throat white, graduating into orange-buff underparts. Dark orange-brown undertail-coverts with white chevrons, orange-brown streaking through hindflanks. Call a short, loud *doid* or *chwit*; song a simple whistling *twee-twee-twee* and trilling notes. Favours woodland and open parkland. Fairly widespread and locally common resident throughout north and central mainland and Lesvos.

WESTERN ROCK NUTHATCH *Sitta neumayer* 13–15cm

Similar in size to Eurasian Nuthatch but with an obviously longer bill and paler, dapper-looking plumage. Upperparts, crown and tail grey-blue. Head pure white below with a narrow black eye-stripe, extending past eye and decurving onto nape. White extends throughout under-parts, with a hint of buff-beige sometimes evident on hindflanks. Song comprises loud, long trills and whistles. Restless, active nuthatch of exposed rocky habitats with scattered trees and bushes, often at altitude. Favours hillside limestone outcrops along coasts and inland. May nest in old buildings; nest a flask-shaped mud structure with a tunnel entrance. Fairly widespread and locally common resident.

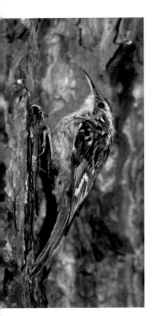

SHORT-TOED TREECREEPER
Certhia brachydactyla 12cm

Small brown-and-white woodland bird with a fine, decurved bill, strong toes and long, stiff tail used to creep up tree trunks and branches. Plumage cryptic against tree bark. Upperparts mid-brown with paler fine streaking throughout. Wings dark brown, peppered with white spots and with sandy-brown fringes forming Z-shaped wing-bar. Tail sandy brown and pointed. Head with short white supercilium, white cheek-patch, minute eye and white throat leading to white underparts. Pale brown wash to hindflanks. In the field, very hard to separate from Eurasian Treecreeper (*C. familiaris*, scarce and local in north; not illustrated). Call a repeated strong *tuut* (Eurasian's is a repetitive thin, piercing *sriii*). Fairly common and very widespread resident of woodlands, parks, gardens.

EURASIAN PENDULINE TIT *Remiz pendulinus* 11cm

Similar in size to Eurasian Blue Tit, with short wings and a rather long tail, the latter much shorter than in Bearded Reedling. Male plumage similar to that of male Red-backed Shrike, with rufous-brown back, rufous spotting to upper breast and peachy-white underparts. Wings feathers dark-centred, with chestnut, buff and grey fringes. Head light grey with broad black face mask and white throat. Bill silvery grey, legs black. Female similar but with narrower black face mask, lighter brown back and no breast spotting. Juvenile has a uniform buff head. Favours scrubby, wooded and marshy wetland fringes, reedbeds, lakesides and tree-lined riverbanks. May gather in small flocks in reedbeds in winter. Nest is an intricately woven tunnel-entranced dome suspended over water. Fairly widespread and locally common resident.

▼ *Adult male*

▼ *Adult at nest*

▲ Adult male   ▲ Adult female

EURASIAN GOLDEN ORIOLE *Oriolus oriolus* 24cm

Surprisingly difficult to see considering its colour and size; look for it on migration, when it occurs in small roaming flocks. Males egg-yolk yellow above and below, including head, contrasting with black wings, tail and lores. Bill chunky and red, legs grey. Female duller, with solid yellow largely replaced by mossy green and paler yellow, underparts white with fine brown streaks and wings browner. Juvenile lichen green above and on wings, white and steaked below. Call a harsh, grating *kyer*; song comprises melodious whistling and yodelling. Prefers open deciduous woodland, poplar plantations and cherry trees. Fairly common and widespread summer visitor and passage migrant, most numerous in spring. Breeds in north and central mainland and on a few islands.

RED-BACKED SHRIKE *Lanius collurio* 17cm

Commonest small shrike. Sturdy, with a strong, hooked black bill and longish tail. Male has chestnut-brown upperparts and wings, grey rump, and black tail with white base. Head ash grey with black face mask and white throat. Underparts creamy, tinted rose-pink. Female upperparts chestnut brown, face plain with brown ear-coverts, underparts whitish with fine barring. Juvenile like female but upperparts also barred. Call a harsh *chip* or *chack*; song a subdued warbling. Perches motionless in the open looking for prey, which may be impaled on thorns for later consumption. Frequents open habitats with scattered trees, bushes, woodland edges and farmland. Common, widespread summer visitor, but does not breed in large parts of south mainland or on most islands; very common passage migrant, especially in autumn.

▼ Adult male   ▼ Adult female

LESSER GREY SHRIKE *Lanius minor* 20cm

Compact shrike with comparatively long wings and a short square tail. Adult ash grey on crown, nape and back, wings black and tail with small square white wing-patch, tail black. Face has a black mask, diagnostically broader at forehead, giving a blunt-headed appearance. Underparts white with a baby-pink flush. Legs and stout bill dark grey. Juvenile similar but with many scaly white feather edges to upperparts and dark barring to crown. Prefers open cultivated areas and dry grassland, rocky terrain with scattered trees and bushes. Fairly widespread but scarce summer visitor and passage migrant, more numerous in autumn. Missing as a breeding bird from central mainland areas and most islands.

138

WOODCHAT SHRIKE *Lanius senator* 18cm

Stocky, large-headed shrike. Male has black upperparts with a white shoulder-patch, fringes on flight feathers and wing-bar, and a white-and-grey rump. Head shows mahogany-brown crown and nape, black face, stubby bill and white throat. Underparts white, flanks with apricot wash, tail black, outer tail white. Female like a washed-out male, dark grey on back, with paler orange-brown crown and nape, and flank barring visible at close range. Juvenile resembles Red-backed Shrike juvenile, but paler brown throughout, rump-patch pale (not chestnut brown) and more white on shoulder. Call a harsh *kiwick*; song varied, musical and scratchy. Prefers open lowland woodland, rocky terrain with scattered trees on which to perch, coastal plains and olive groves. Common and widespread summer visitor.

MASKED SHRIKE *Lanius nubicus* 17–18cm

Slender shrike with a finer bill and much longer tail than other shrikes. Upperparts black from crown to tail base, with contrasting white shoulder-panel, wing-patch, fringes to flight feathers and outer tail. Head has black mask stripe from eye to black hindcrown. Forehead, lores and supercilium white; throat white, leading onto white underparts, these with extensive apricot tones, particularly along flanks and hindflanks. Female similar but dark grey above and with reduced apricot on flanks. Juvenile like a monochrome adult, grey and white above and uniform white below. Call a harsh *tsr*; song a burst of warbling and scratchy notes. Frequents open woodland, countryside with scattered trees and bushes, and cultivated areas. Scarce local summer visitor to north-east mainland and larger islands.

EURASIAN JAY *Garrulus glandarius* 34–35cm

Large, well-built, colourful corvid with a shy, alarmist nature. Upperparts pinkish grey through hindcrown, nape and back. Large white rump-patch, long all-black tail. Wings black with white wing-patch, pale fringes to flight feathers, and dazzling blue-and-black chequered wing-panel. Head with fine black streaking to white crown, dusky-pink face with pale eye, and short, broad sub-moustachial stripe. Underparts dusky pink with white undertail-coverts and vent. Bill strong and grey, legs sturdy and pink. Alarm call a loud, harsh screech. Prefers orchards, olive groves and dense woodlands, especially with oaks for their acorns. Widespread and locally common resident. Five races occur; *G. g. graecus* is most common throughout the mainland, and *G. g. anatoliae* (with a black crown) occurs on Lesvos.

COMMON MAGPIE
Pica pica 44–46cm

Very distinctive long-bodied black-and-white crow with an extremely long tail and bold disposition. Plumage all black from head to tail-tip, aside from elongated white wing-panel and well-defined large white belly-patch. In good light, a purple-blue gloss can be seen on black flight feathers and forest-green gloss to black tail. Alarm call a loud, fast, scratchy *tcha-tcha-tcha-tcha-tcha*. Frequents open countryside, cultivated areas with scattered trees and bushes, olive groves, areas of human habitation and roadsides. Common and widespread resident, but absent from nearly all islands.

ALPINE CHOUGH *Pyrrhocorax graculus* 38cm

Similar in size to Western Jackdaw, but slender-bodied, with a small head and longer tail. Smaller and with a shorter bill and legs than Red-billed Chough. Adult has uniform black plumage throughout. Bill slightly decurved and yellow (not unlike that of male Common Blackbird), legs short and red. In flight, shows short 'fingers' to primaries, and dark coverts and body contrast with greyer flight feathers and tail. Call a piercing high-pitched *chree*. Highly gregarious and often confiding; can form large roving, aerobatic flocks year-round. Prefers steep stony habitats with short vegetation. Fairly widespread and locally common resident of the highest alpine zones in mainland and on Crete.

▼ *Adults*   ▶ *In flight*

RED-BILLED CHOUGH *Pyrrhocorax pyrrhocorax* 39–40cm

Stunning mountain corvid with glossy black plumage, a long red bill and rather long red legs. Bill is much longer and more distinctly decurved than in Alpine Chough (although note juvenile bill is dull yellow and shorter than in adult); in flight, primaries deeply 'fingered' in comparison. Call a loud *chwee-ou*, not unlike that of Western Jackdaw but higher pitched. Often confiding and gregarious, except when breeding, and can form large aerobatic flocks. Favours slopes with short vegetation; not confined to highest alpine habitats like Alpine Chough, descending to lower altitudes in winter. Fairly widespread but scarce resident, much more localised than Alpine Chough but found on several islands.

WESTERN JACKDAW *Corvus monedula* 33–34cm

Smaller than Hooded Crow and Rook, and more compact, stockier and shorter-tailed than similar-sized choughs. Adult appears all black at a distance, but close views reveal pale grey to 'shawl' area across hindcrown, neck and nape, and varying amounts of grey on mantle and upper breast. Eye pale and very obvious. Feathering around nostrils. In flight, underwing clearly uniform grey. Juvenile all black. Pairs up during the breeding season, but forms large flocks in winter and roosts communally. Call a distinctive *chack*. Primarily a lowland species, favouring gorges, ravines, and rocky inland and coastal habitats. Nests in old rural buildings. Common and widespread resident over most of mainland, patchily distributed in far south and absent from many islands.

▼ *Adult* ▼ *Adult in nest*

▲ Adult

▲ Adult in flight

ROOK *Corvus frugilegus* 44–46cm

Large black corvid, similar in size to Hooded Crow but with a longer, straighter bill and more angled crown. Adult best identified by bare, pale grey skin around base of bill, reaching eye, and lack of feathers on nostrils. Plumage black with glossy purple-blue sheen visible in good light, feathers rather dishevelled and loose around upper legs. Juvenile lacks bare grey face at bill base; bill and head shape best features to separate it from Hooded Crow. Call a very croaky, flat *kaah* or *graah*, often repeated. Frequents farmland, agricultural areas and open countryside with scattered trees, especially near villages and towns. Fairly widespread and locally very common winter visitor to north, often in flocks with Western Jackdaws.

HOODED CROW *Corvus cornix* 45–47cm

Large black-and-grey crow, easily distinguished from other corvids. Head, breast, thighs, wings and tail are black, set against pale grey (almost mauve-grey in some light) on rest of body. Bill dark grey, short and deep, with slightly curved upper mandible. Legs dark grey. Call a hard, croaky burst of repeated *kraa* notes. Found in a wide variety of habitats and altitudes. Not as gregarious as other corvids, but will readily gather with Western Jackdaws and Rooks in winter. The most common and widespread corvid over the mainland and most islands.

▲ Adult

▲ Adult in flight

NORTHERN RAVEN *Corvus corax* 64cm

Bulky, powerfully built corvid, very distinctive on size and shape alone. Plumage all black with hint of a blue-green sheen in good light. Very heavy, deep bill dominates head and is obvious at a distance, even in flight, with neat curve to front of upper mandible and beard-like throat feathers adding to front-heavy appearance. In flight, obvious diamond-shaped fanned tail eases identification, as do long narrow wings. Call a deep, low, croaky *prrrk* or repeated *krark-krark-krark*. Found across lowland and high montane habitats. Fairly common and widespread resident throughout.

COMMON STARLING *Sturnus vulgaris* 21cm

Smaller, more slender and shorter-tailed than Common Blackbird, with a longer, finer, pointed yellow bill and gangly pink legs. Summer adult black with an iridescent purple-green sheen. Winter adult has striking plumage of white and buff spots/chevrons to feather tips throughout, and brown edges to flight feathers. Bill becomes dark, legs dull pink. Juvenile all brown-grey, bill dark grey. First-winter soon resembles winter adult, but with head often remaining brown-grey. Unlike Common Blackbird, very fidgety and active, often running along ground. Forms impressive murmurations in winter. Prefers agricultural habitats, olive groves, coastal plains, and urban and suburban habitats. Fairly common but local resident in north; very common, familiar and widespread winter visitor throughout.

▼ Adult

▼ Adult in flight

ROSY STARLING *Pastor roseus* 21cm

Very like Common Starling in structure and behaviour, but plumage very different. Adult has a distinct pink mantle, back, rump, lower breast and belly, contrasting with glossy black head, throat, upper breast, wings and tail. Crown has a long, drooping black crest. Bill and legs dull pinkish. Juvenile similar to Common Starling juvenile, but wings blackish and bill base yellow. First-winter like adult but washed out, with grey mottling to pink plumage. Favours open agricultural areas with scattered trees. Irregular, rare breeding species in colonies in stone quarries in north; fairly widespread passage migrant to most of mainland and some larger islands. Often seen in small roving flocks in June.

HOUSE SPARROW *Passer domesticus* 14–15cm

Familiar small, compact, stout-billed species. Male has grey crown and face-sides, broad chestnut band from eye to nape, and black bib and lores. Upperparts brown with black streaks and white wing-bar. Underparts uniform grey. Female and juvenile similar but paler brown, lacking facial markings and with only faint buff supercilium on greyish-brown crown. Call an uplifting *chirp*. Frequents villages, towns, rural settlements and farmland. Nests in loose colonies; can build domed nests but prefers holes in buildings and in the side of White Stork nests when available. Forms large post-breeding flocks that rove agricultural areas by day and roost together in tall trees in towns at night. Very common and widespread resident.

▼ *Adult male*

▼ *Adult female*

SPANISH SPARROW *Passer hispaniolensis* 15cm

Very similar to House Sparrow, but generally more rural. Summer male with chestnut-brown crown, white face-sides, broken white supercilium, and black lores and eye-stripe. Throat black; underparts white with black chevron streaking, heaviest along flanks. Upperparts with black chevron streaks to mantle; wings chestnut brown with white wing-bar. Winter male has reduced black markings but chevron streaking still visible. Female and juvenile resemble their House Sparrow counterparts. Favours rural fringes around human settlements and agricultural areas. Nests in trees, orchards, small copses and near White Stork nests. Forms huge roving flocks post-breeding. Locally very common resident and summer visitor with a patchy yet widespread distribution. Northern birds migrate south in impressive numbers in autumn.

EURASIAN TREE SPARROW *Passer montanus* 14cm

The least common *Passer* sparrow in Greece. Smaller, neater and slimmer than House and Spanish sparrows. Adult easily identified by chestnut-brown crown, small black bib, lores and eye surround, and obvious black cheek-spot in white face. Upperparts chestnut to mid-brown, with black streaking and a white wing-bar. Underparts pale grey throughout. Juvenile has a reduced black cheek-patch on grey face. Call an upbeat *tschirp*. Prefers farmland, towns, villages, olive groves and orchards. Nests in tree-holes. Forms small post-breeding flocks, sometimes mixed with House Sparrow and common finches. Fairly widespread and locally common resident. Distribution not fully known, but numerous across Macedonia and Thrace in the north and the Peloponnese in the south.

ROCK SPARROW *Petronia petronia* 14cm

Larger and longer-winged than *Passer* sparrows, with a bigger head, chunky conical bill and pink lower mandible. Head with a distinctive, pale buff supercilium; dark-bordered pale crown-stripe; and dark eye-stripe. Upperparts tawny brown with intricate grey, brown, black and white patterning to wing and dark streaks along mantle. Tail with diagnostic white spots on tips, obvious in flight. Underparts cream with brown streaking, denser along flanks. Call a piercing *peeyuee*. Runs like a pipit. Bird of open stony hillsides, dry grassland, quarries and rock faces. Nests colonially in rock crevices and old buildings. Can form large, noisy flocks. Fairly widespread but scarce resident, mainly in Macedonia and Thrace in the north and the Peloponnese further south.

COMMON CHAFFINCH *Fringilla coelebs* 14–15cm

Familiar finch, the size of a sparrow but with a slimmer body and longer tail. Male has a grey-blue crown, nape, shoulder-patch and tail, reddish-brown back, and black-and-white wings with obvious double wing-bar. Forehead shows black patch above bill; face and underparts dusky pink (brightest in summer), and undertail white. Green-grey rump and white outer-tail feathers obvious in flight. Female and juvenile have similar wing and tail pattern, but upperparts and head dull grey-brown, paler on face, and underparts pale brown-grey to white. Call a distinctive *chink*; song an upbeat *chip and chink*, fast and high, descending in a low flourish. Prefers open woodlands, parks, gardens, orchards and farmland. In winter, often in mixed flocks. Very common and widespread resident and winter visitor.

▼ *Adult male*

▼ *Adult female*

▲ Autumn male ▲ Autumn female

BRAMBLING *Fringilla montifringilla* 14cm

Similar to Common Chaffinch in size and shape, but with close views plumage obviously different. Summer male has black head and bill; burnt-orange throat, shoulder and upper breast; and white underparts with black flank spots. Winter male and female show dark-sided brownish-grey face, streaky-buff upperparts, orangey breast, dark-spotted hindflanks and dark-tipped yellow bill; male can show black speckling to head. Wing pattern like that of Common Chaffinch but with buff-orange to whitish wing-bars. In flight, diagnostic white rump aids differentiation from green-grey rump of Common Chaffinch. Call a nasally *wayeek*; flight call a harsh *yeck* or *chucc*. Favours beech-mast and ground seed. Frequents ploughed fields and farmland, often in mixed finch flocks. Fairly common and widespread winter visitor, numbers fluctuating annually.

EUROPEAN SERIN *Serinus serinus* 11cm

Very small, streaked finch with a tiny stout bill. Male has canary-yellow head and underparts, with dark streaks on crown and brownish cheeks. Flanks white with dark streaking. Upperparts green-brown with dark streaks; wings dark with paler feather fringes, creating faint double wing-bars. In flight, shows conspicuous yellow rump-patch. Female similar but duller yellow-brown and streaked on head and underparts. Juvenile mainly streaky brown-buff with finely streaked white underparts. Call a high-pitched, buzzing trill; song a fast, high, almost electrical jingling (identification straightforward on these alone). Prefers open woodland, orchards and olive groves. Nests in high conifers. Locally common, widespread resident over much of the mainland, the Peloponnese and some larger islands.

▲ Adult male

▲ Adult female

EUROPEAN GREENFINCH *Carduelis chloris* 15cm

Large, heavy, thickset finch with a strong bill. Male moss green on back, mantle and shoulders; wings grey and black with vibrant yellow on outer edges of primaries and tail. Rump yellowish green. Head plain grey-green with dark lores and a yellowish bib. Underparts green-yellow with grey flanks and a white undertail. Bill and legs pale pink. Female similar but duller and browner, with faint streaking to brownish-grey back and greyer underparts. Juvenile like female, but underparts whiter with fine grey streaks. Call a twittering *chichichichichit*. Found in mixed open woodland, orchards, large gardens, and farmland with scattered trees. Common and widespread resident.

EUROPEAN GOLDFINCH *Carduelis carduelis* 12cm

Small, rather delicate finch. Adult unmistakable, with red facial disc (extending past top of eye in male) surrounded by broad white band, and black cap and nape collar. Bill pale pink, pointed. Upperparts mushroom brown; wings and tail black with large white spots at feather tips and obvious golden-yellow panel in wing, very clear when perched or in flight. Black-and-yellow wings diagnostic in all ages. Underparts whitish with mushroom-brown wash to flanks and breast. Juvenile has plain brownish head, and streaky back, breast and flanks. Call an upbeat *tirilitt*; song a twittering jangle. Highly gregarious in winter. Common and widespread resident of open woodland, orchards, farmland with scattered copses, gardens and tall grassland.

▲ *Adult male* ▲ *Adult female*

EURASIAN SISKIN *Carduelis spinus* 12cm

Small, short-tailed finch with a relatively long, pointed bill. Male bright with a black crown and bib (reduced in winter), and yellow face, collar and breast. Back grey-green with dark streaking. In flight, yellow rump-patch obvious. Wings black with broad yellow wing-bar. Underparts yellow, whiter towards belly and with dark flank streaks. Tail black and yellow. Female duller grey-green with light streaking on upperparts and head, and pale yellow on plain face, wing-panel, rump and tail. White below with flank streaking. Juvenile like female but paler, with more streaking above and below. Call a whistling two-note *teeyu-tsoooee*; song a high trill. Found in coniferous and mixed woodland. Rare local resident in north mainland mountains; fairly common and widespread winter visitor, often in roving flocks.

COMMON LINNET *Carduelis cannabina* 13cm

Small, slender, long-tailed finch with a stout grey bill. Summer male striking, with a rose-red forehead and breast, grey head and throat, reddish-chestnut upperparts, and black-and-white wings and tail. Underparts below breast white with brown wash to flanks. Winter male duller, reddish upperparts diffused. Female duller, with mid-brown upperparts, greyer-brown head, finely streaked buff-brown throat and breast, white belly, and similar black and white on wings and tail. Juvenile resembles female but with more streaking throughout. Call an upbeat *tigg-it* or a twittering *kekeke-keke*; song a lively mix of twitters and trills. Prefers open countryside, farmland with hedgerows, scrub and bush-rich habitats. In winter, forms large flocks in saltmarshes and agricultural areas. Common and widespread resident.

▼ *Adult male* ▼ *Adult female*

▲ Adult variations   ▲ Adult

RED CROSSBILL *Loxia curvirostra* 16cm

Larger than European Greenfinch but with a similarly robust structure, large head and short tail. Bill chunky and broad-based, but distinctly pointed, overlapping and crossed near tip. Tail sharply forked (more obvious in flight). Male plumage varies from red-orange to yellow-green (more common in Greece), with darker dusky wings and tail. Female variable grey-green to dull yellow, with dusky wings and tail. Both show obvious yellow, orange or red rump depending on colour of individual. Juvenile grey-green to brown, heavily streaked. Very vocal, call a distinct, repeated metallic *jip-jip-jip*. Dependent on the cones of upland pines. Fairly widespread but scarce resident with a patchy distribution across montane areas of mainland; can be common and more widespread in invasion years.

EURASIAN BULLFINCH *Pyrrhula pyrrhula* 16cm

Unobtrusive rotund finch with a bull neck and chubby black bill. Male has a black cap extending over front of face and bill, black wings with a broad white wing-bar, and black tail. Mantle and back pale grey, face and underparts bright pink-red, rump and undertail white. Female similar but with grey-brown face and underparts. Juvenile has plain grey-brown head with no black, otherwise like female. Call a rather mournful, low, whistling *phew*. Frequents scrub and open mixed woodland, thickets and orchards, often in mountains. Scarce local resident with a patchy north mainland breeding distribution; scarce winter visitor with a distinctly northern bias.

▼ Adult male   ▼ Adult female

HAWFINCH *Coccothraustes coccothraustes* 17cm

Stocky finch with a large head, thick neck, chunky bill and short tail. Male dark brown on back, with a grey neck collar and orange-brown head, rump and tail. Lores and bib black, set around conical grey bill. Wings blackish with a white wing-panel and broad, glossy blue-black inner primaries. Underparts pale pink-buff with white undertail and broad white tail-tip. Female similar but duller; shows grey panel to secondaries and lacks blue-black inner primaries. Juvenile has a greyish breast and dark belly spotting. In flight, all birds appear front heavy and show obvious white in wings and tail. Call a loud, hard metallic *tick*. Prefers deciduous woodland for breeding, and open woodland, scrub, orchards and farmland copses in winter. Fairly widespread but scarce resident across north; widespread and locally common winter visitor.

YELLOWHAMMER *Emberiza citrinella* 16cm

Large, long-tailed bunting with a neat grey bill. Summer male chestnut brown above with black streaking and unmarked chestnut-brown rump. Wings and tail with dark feathers edged chestnut brown. Head and underparts striking yellow, with dark marks to cheek and crown. Breast and flanks rusty brown, the latter with fine dark streaking. Female and winter male similar but duller, head and underparts muted yellow, greyer brown above and heavily streaked below. Juvenile much greyer brown above and on head, with only a tinge of yellow below, if any. Call a hard *tzit* and more liquid *pitilip*. Fairly common but local upland resident; locally common winter visitor to north and centre. In summer, occurs in montane woodland clearing and scrub; in winter, mixed flocks gather on farmland, open countryside and coastal lowlands.

▲ Adult male
▼ Adult female

▲ *Adult male*

▲ *Adult female*

CIRL BUNTING *Emberiza cirlus* 16cm

Slightly smaller and more compact than Yellowhammer. Male boldly patterned, black throat and eye-stripe contrasting with yellow face and narrow yellow neck band. Broad breast-band, nape and crown olive green, underparts yellow, lower breast-sides brown with dark streaking to flanks. Upperparts chestnut brown with dark streaking, wings with pale-edged black-centred feathers. Female and juvenile best separated from Yellowhammer counterparts on rump, which is olive-grey, and on face pattern, which shows well-defined dark facial stripes on cleaner face. Juvenile also whiter below. Call a short, thin *tzip*; song a rattling *zezezeze* like that of Lesser Whitethroat. Prefers field margins, open grassland with scattered trees, bushes, farmland with copses, hedgerows, olive groves and orchards. Common, widespread resident.

ROCK BUNTING *Emberiza cia* 16cm

Slender, long-tailed bunting with distinctive coloration and detail. Male head, neck, breast and shoulder-patch dove grey, face with contrasting narrow black lateral crown-stripe, eye-stripe and cheek surround. Upperparts red-brown with black streaking along back, and black-centred wing feathers with red-brown edges. Rump unmarked, red-brown; tail red-brown with obvious white outer-tail feathers. Female similar but duller. Juvenile duller and streaky. Calls include a sharp *tsi* or *zeet*; song , frequently from treetops, varied, high-pitched and melodic. Prefers dry, open montane habitat around treeline, with rocky areas and scattered scrub, bushes and trees. Often moves to lowlands in winter. Fairly widespread but scarce resident. Breeds only on mainland, but with a rather patchy distribution.

CINEREOUS BUNTING *Emberiza cineracea* 16–17cm

Rather plain, slender, long-tailed bunting. Male greyish above with faint dark back streaking and white outer-tail feathers. Wing feathers black with pale tawny-brown and white edges. Face yellow-grey with a green hue, white eye-ring and pale grey bill. Throat yellow; underparts clean grey, white on underbelly. Female similar but yellow on face and throat replaced with buff-grey and underparts finely streaked. Juvenile like female but buff-white below, with breast and flank streaking. Call a metallic *cup*; song a simple *zru-zru-zru-zru-zru-zru*. Resident of dry stony slopes and open hillsides with low scrub. Extremely rare, local summer visitor to Lesvos, Chios and Skyros. Greece and Turkey are home to more than 90 per cent of the global population.

ORTOLAN BUNTING *Emberiza hortulana* 16cm

Rather shy, slender bunting with a long tail and pastel-coloured plumage. Male has a green-grey head, neck and upper breast, contrasting with yellow-cream throat, sub-moustachial stripe and eye-ring. Upperpart feathers dark-centred with tawny-brown fringes. Underparts orange-brown. Bill and legs pink. Female and juvenile similar but duller throughout, with head, neck and upper breast diffuse grey-brown and streaked. Call commonly a *sli-e*, often followed by *tseu*, also a flat *plett* when disturbed; song varied, simple, often with repeated high notes followed by lower-pitched notes or one longer note. Widespread, locally common summer visitor to mainland and some islands. Occurs in varied habitats, from open scrubby, rocky terrain and agricultural areas at lower altitudes, to more mountainous forest edges and clearings.

▼ *Adult male*

▼ *Juvenile/first winter*

CRETZSCHMAR'S BUNTING *Emberiza caesia* 16cm

Similar to slightly larger Ortolan Bunting, but with subtle yet obvious colour differences. Male coloration brighter than in Ortolan, with grey-blue head, neck and upper breast, warmer brown upperparts and deeper orange-brown underparts. Key identification features are rusty-brown throat and sub-moustachial stripe, and white eye-ring. Female and juvenile duller, like Ortolan counterparts, but with washed-out rusty-brown tones above and below, particularly on face. Call similar to Ortolan's but sharper; song also similar but thinner, with less ringing quality. Prefers dry, open rocky hillsides with scrub and bushes, from low to high altitudes. Fairly widespread, locally common summer visitor to south and central mainland and some islands.

COMMON REED BUNTING *Emberiza schoeniclus* 16cm

Smallest bunting in Greece. Summer male brown above with dark streaks along back and brown-edged dark-centred wing feathers. White neck collar and sub-moustachial stripe contrast with solid black head, throat and upper central breast. In flight, white underparts and outer-tail feathers obvious. In winter male, black head markings become diffuse and paler brown. Female and juvenile similar, but with complex head pattern of greyish-brown collar, streaked brown crown, blackish malar stripe, and broad buff supercilium, sub-moustachial stripe and chin. Underparts off-white to buff, heavily streaked. Call a downslurred *siiuu*. Frequents wetlands, marshes and farmlands. Scarce local resident of reedbeds and wetlands in north; common and widespread winter visitor throughout, often in mixed flocks.

▼ *Adult male*

▼ *Adult female*

▲ Adult male

▲ Adult female

BLACK-HEADED BUNTING *Emberiza melanocephala* 16–17cm

Very familiar, colourful bunting with a rather brazen nature. Male has a chestnut-brown back and rump, solid black hood, and canary-yellow throat, collar and underparts. Wings feathers dark, edged pale brown and white, forming a double wing-bar. Female very washed out in comparison, with a greyish hood, grey-brown upperparts and faint yellow underparts. Juvenile similar to female but more streaked above and paler buff below, with only a hint of yellow on throat and underparts. Call like that of Ortolan Bunting; song a rhythmic, jangling rattle, often from a high, exposed perch. Favours open farmland and countryside with scattered trees, bushes and hedgerows. Widespread and locally very common summer visitor, but rare in Crete.

CORN BUNTING *Emberiza calandra* 18cm

Very plain, robust bunting with a chunky bill. Grey-brown above with dark streaking through crown, nape and back. Wings have dark-centred feathers, edged pale grey-brown. Underparts whitish with dark streaks throughout, densely clustered in centre of breast. Face plain grey-brown with paler sub-moustachial stripe bordering darker ear-coverts. Bill heavy, with paler yellowish lower mandible. Call a short *bitt* or metallic *tsritt*; song a distinct short, jangling rattle rather like a pocketful of jingling keys. Male often sings from natural perches or telegraph wires in spring. Favours open countryside, farmland with scattered trees, bushes and hedgerows, and dry grassland. Very common and widespread resident throughout. Most numerous in winter, when large flocks form on lowland farmland.

GLOSSARY

Bib The area covering the throat and at least part of the upper breast.

Carpal patch An area, usually distinctly pale or dark, at the bend of the upper wing. Often evident in certain birds of prey (raptor) species.

Crest A concentration of feathers on top of a bird's head.

Ear-coverts Feathered area behind and slightly below eye at the cheek.

Ear-tufts A concentration of longer feathers on top of the head and above each eye in certain species, such as owls.

Eclipse Temporary, dull, post-summer plumage moult stage in male ducks.

Eye-stripe A line, usually dark, running either side of the eye.

Gape The fleshy area of skin bridging a bird's upper and lower mandible at the base of the bill. Often enlarged in young birds.

Hindflanks The flank section closest to the tail end of the bird.

Immature No longer a juvenile but still young, not yet having attained full adult plumage.

Lores The small area between the bill base and eye of all birds.

Malar stripe A stripe, often dark, running down a birds face, from the base of the lower mandible down through the edge of the throat.

Moustachial stripe A fine stripe, often dark, running down and across the lower cheek from the base of the upper mandible.

Morph A variation in colour in adult plumage of some species. Usually a pale and dark phase or light and dark version exist.

Nape (or **Hindneck**) The back of a bird's neck.

Passage migrant Only passing through during migration, from summering to wintering grounds and vice versa.

Plumes Special feathers displayed by some birds during courtship and the breeding season for increased attractiveness.

Primary feathers/primaries The outermost flight feathers on a bird's wing.

Resident A bird that lives in a particular area all year round.

Secondary feathers/secondaries The innermost flight feathers on a bird's wing, also known as the 'hand' of the wing.

Speculum A patch of plumage, often bright, on most ducks' secondary wing feathers. Often visible when wings are closed as well as in flight.

Sub-moustachial stripe A fine stripe, often pale, running down the lower cheek from the bill base in beween the moustachial stripe and malar stripe.

Trailing edge The outer edge of a bird's wing, visible in flight.

Underbelly The area between the belly and the legs.

Underparts The bottom section of a bird, usually encompassing throat, breast, belly, flanks, underside of wings and underside of tail.

Underwing The underneath area of the wing.

Upperparts The top section of a bird, usually encompassing crown, neck, nape, mantle, back, rump, upperside of wings and upperside of tail.

Upperwing The top area of the wing.

Wing-bar A distinctive coloured (usually white or dark) stripe, forming a bar across a bird's upper wing. Often evident at rest as well as in flight.

Wing coverts Groups, or layers of feathers that overlay the primaries and secondaries on the wing, the primary and secondary coverts. These are also defined in more detail as greater, median and lesser coverts that overlap each other on a bird's wing.

PHOTO CREDITS

All of the photographs in this book were taken by Rebecca Nason, with the exception of the following:

Eyal Bartov/Alamy: 93B; Gary Bell: 73T; Szymon Bartosz/Alamy: 94B; Klaus Bjerre/NPL: 45TR, 51TR; Oliver Born/Alamy: 21B; Philip Harris: 110T; Chris Gomersall: 22T, 29T, 35BL, 35BR, 36BL, 36BR, 37BL, 37BR, 40BR, 46T, 47BR, 61T, 97T, 109BL, 152TL, 152TR; Mike Lane/Alamy: 155TR; Philip Newman/NPL: 41TL, 41ML; Danielle Occhiato/Alamy: 26B, 107T; David Tipling: 11T, 23TR, 31B, 32BR, 36R, 37TL, 38BL, 38BR, 39BL, 44TL, 44TR, 47BL, 50BR, 51BL, 52T, 53B, 55B, 57B, 65BL, 70TR, 75BR, 79BR, 82T, 86T, 87T, 88T, 98BL, 100BR, 103T, 103BL, 104TL, 104BL, 105B, 110BL, 116B, 118T, 121BL, 123B, 127B, 131B, 141T, 147B, 149BL; Babis & Sakis Tsilianidis: 23B, 25TL, 25TR, 25BR, 28T, 28B, 32BL, 43TR, 44B, 45B, 51TL, 60TL, 60TR, 61B, 65T, 72T, 75TL, 75TR, 78B, 78TL, 79TL, 80T, 83T, 93T, 95B, 98T, 101T, 103BR, 109T, 112B, 116T, 117T, 117B, 118BL, 118BR, 120BL, 120BR, 125T, 135B, 136BL, 136BR, 137BL, 152B; Roger Riddington: 101B, 121T; Paul Sterry/NPL: 20BL, 21T, 22B, 25BL, 35TL, 36TL, 39TL, 39BR, 42TL, 42TM, 42TR, 42BL, 42BR, 43BL, 45TL, 51BL, 52B, 53T, 58BL, 67T, 71T, 76T, 78TR, 91TR, 96T, 111TL, 111TR, 113T, 119TL, 119TR, 120T, 122T, 124T, 126T, 129B, 130T, 132T, 136T, 137TL, 137TR, 138T, 144T, 153T; Rory Tallack: 26TL, 26TR, 27TL, 83B, 92, 128B; Brydon Thomason: 50TL; Roger Tidman/NPL: 36B, 40BL, 41BR, 47TL, 47TR, 95T, 138B, 146T.

RESOURCES

Dudley, S. 2009. *A Birdwatching Guide to Lesvos*. Arlequin Press, Shrewsbury.

Handrinos, G. and Akriotis, T. 1997. *The Birds of Greece*. Christopher Helm, London.

Mills, S. 2011. *Birdwatching in Northern Greece: A Site Guide*. 2nd edn. Birdwing Books, Whitby.

Snow, D.W. and Perrins, C.M. 1997. *The Birds of the Western Palearctic. Vols 1 and 2*. Concise edn. Oxford University Press, Oxford.

Svensson, L., Mullarney, K. and Zetterstrom, D. 2009. *Collins Bird Guide*. 2nd edn. HarperCollins, London.

Vlachos, C., Trigou, R. and Stavrakas, L. 2014. *Birding in Greece. A Travel Guide to Birdwatching Sites in Greece*. 2nd edn. Hellenic Ornithological Society, Athens.

Welch, H., Rose, L., Moore, D., Oddie, B. and Sigg, H. 1996. *Where to Watch Birds in Turkey, Greece and Cyprus*. Hamlyn Birdwatching Guides in association with BirdLife International, London.

ACKNOWLEDGEMENTS

Rebecca wishes to thank Jim Martin (Bloomsbury) for his confidence in commissioning the book, and Molly Arnold (Bloomsbury) for guiding the book's production from start to finish, as well as Susi Bailey for her excellent editing skills. Thanks to Phil and daughter Ayda Ruby for their patience and for allowing her time to write, Denise and Steve Nason for proofreading, Deryk and Hollie Shaw for their encouragement and various photographers for granting use of their wonderful images.

INDEX